Death, Transcendence, and Beyond:

A Priest's Psychopomp Journey into the Reality of the Afterlife

by Rev. Gary W. Duncan, M.S., M.A., CSM/OCP

DORRANCE
PUBLISHING CO
EST. 1920
PITTSBURGH, PENNSYLVANIA 15238

Dorrance Publishing Co
585 Alpha Drive
Suite 103
Pittsburgh, PA 15238
Visit our website at *www.dorrancebookstore.com*

ISBN: 979-8-88925-989-3
eISBN: 979-8-89127-102-9

Death, Transcendence, and Beyond:

A Priest's Psychopomp Journey into the Reality of the Afterlife

"We can control only what is inferior to us and that any discipline that studies solely what is subject to control and limitation cannot reveal anything transcendent—i.e., superior to us in intelligence, awareness, compassion, or any other criterion of worth."

Huston Smith (1992)

"There is no salvation in becoming adapted to a world which is crazy."

Henry Miller

"Just look at us. Everything is backwards, everything is upside down. Doctors destroy health, lawyers destroy justice, psychiatrists destroy minds, scientists destroy truth, major media destroys information, religions destroy spirituality and governments destroy freedom."

Michael Ellner

"The Dark Ages still reign over all Humanity, and the cause of this domination is now becoming clear. The Dark Ages Prison has no steel bars or locks. Instead, it is locked by misorientation and misinformation created by the human Ego. People are intractably skeptical of what they do not understand. We are powerfully imprisoned in these Dark Ages simply by the terms in which we have been conditioned to think."

Buckminster Fuller

"It is difficult to make a man understand something when his salary depends upon his not understanding it."

Upton Sinclair

DEDICATION

This book is dedicated to the Charon or Kharon the first psychopomp who charged money for his services.

In the tradition of Greek mythology, Charon is a man who lives in the Underworld. He is the son of Erebus and Nyx, and it is his responsibility to ferry the dead between the world of the living and the Underworld, across the River Styx. In some myths, he carries the dead over the river Acheron, the "river of woe." Charon appears in numerous stories, plays, and myths, and a version of him lives on in Greek folklore as an angel of death.

Charon's services do not come gratis with death. Although Hermes may have taken the souls of the dead to the banks of the river for free, Charon demands his fee. People who are unable to pay the fee are doomed to wander the shores of the river for 100 years. Since most Greeks, understandably, did not want to wander in the mists and marshes, they buried their dead with coins to pay the ferryman; this tradition is still retained in many parts of Greece.

Depictions of Charon vary. In some cases, he is said to be an old man with a twisted body and a bitter attitude, while in other instances, he is a horned demon with a formidable hammer. The portrayal of Charon as a skeleton in a robe is primarily a modern invention. In many myths, he also hurls insults or makes sour statements about the deceased. Many religions include a figure like Charon, a representative of death and the Underworld, suggesting to followers that there is life after death, and that people require proper preparations for death.

Living people who want to visit Hades must also pay the ferryman. Given the fact that they need two trips, Charon charges significantly more, and several myths and stories indicate that visitors to Hades pay with a golden branch to cross the river with Charon and return. Several Greek and Roman authors wrote about traveling to the Underworld, usually with the assistance of an experienced guide. Dante, for example, wrote *The Inferno*, and the *Aeneid* by Virgil also features a trip to the Underworld.

Incidentally, for anyone concerned about paying the ferryman, his going rate in Ancient Greece was an obolus, a silver coin worth a sixth of a drachma. Since Greece has now switched over to the euro, along with other members of the European Union, Charon would probably accept a euro coin, and he may be open to other currencies as well.

In Greek Mythology, Who Is Charon? http://www.wisegeek.com/in-greek-mythology-who-is-charon.htm. Wise Geek

Name Disclaimer

Most of the names in this book have been changed to protect identity.

ACKNOWLEDGEMENTS

I am honored to all those with AIDS I helped go through the dying process and into the afterlife.

I thank all those who participated in the guided imagery experience into the light.

I thank all those who participated in the After Death Communication imagery.

I thank Daryl I. Coston, Marquita Asher, Jeffrey Eaddy, and Tim Collins for reading the first draft and making suggestions on how to make the narrative a better read.

A special thanks to the editors of *New Dawn Magazine* for allowing me to write articles from the books content to advertise the book when it is published.

Table of Contents

INTRODUCTION

There have been five streams that have formed the foundation of my life's journey: spirituality, religion, magick, science and sexuality. All these areas I explored in-depth and found the experiences were relevant to understanding the reality around me. I knew early on I had to keep my explorations, experiments and discoveries secret because of society's violent reactions and blind ignorance to what I was doing—I simply could not trust anyone. However, over the years my secret discoveries brought me to a profound awakening to what reality appears to be.

Of the five streams, the spiritual was the main driving force that propelled me into uncovering the depth of my soul's journeys in this reality as well as other realities. In childhood, I learned pagan rituals from my maternal grandmother setting the stage for my exploration into death, reincarnation, karma, near-death-experience, the afterlife and magick, preparing me to become a psychotherapist, a spiritual psychopomp, and an Ordained Priest.

Up until my teens, my understanding of the spiritual was what my maternal grandmother taught me. She was a pagan Christian with Celtic, Druid, Cherokee and magickal influences. She believed the spirit and the soul were in everything. Her view of the soul was very different from what Christianity had to offer. During this period, I understood the soul and the spirit from both my grandmother's and the Christian perspectives. My sophomore year of high school ushered in two new concepts my grandmother, nor the Christians ever taught me: reincarnation and karma.

When I first encountered these concepts, I was intrigued but soon felt there was something wrong with these ideas. Reincarnation and karma didn't make sense because some people I knew believed that their current problems were the result of some transgressions in some other past lifetime. Some believed they were the reincarnation of historical figures both great and of lesser status and the problems those figures had were affecting the person's current life. What I found intriguing was these people always returned to the planet Earth to work through the karmic debt of what those historical figures supposed to have done.

I puzzled, why these souls always reincarnate back to the planet Earth? Why do some people supposedly come back as some great historic figure, and some don't? Aren't there other planets in our universe with intelligent beings we could have been incarnated from. In addition, aren't there other realities we could be incarnated from. In all the years I performed past-life regression, I had only one person coming from an alternate reality. Except for that one case, all the reincarnation and past life stories I've heard are all centered on the planet Earth—something is wrong with this idea. Why would a soul keep coming back over and over to this ignorant, violent, and uncivilized planet?

Not only did I have problems with reincarnation but also karma as well. Karma has always felt like another form of retribution such as sin; neither concept made sense if one believes in a loving compassionate god. And why would a so-called merciful, loving, and compassionate god punish people anyway? Based on my life experiences, I came to understand that rather than karma or sin shaping our lives it was free will choices and the resulting consequences, which is the best measure influencing our soul's destiny.

Free will choices is the engine that would bring a soul back to the planet Earth and not some frivolous concept called karma, which by the way appears more relevant to Eastern religions. Reincarnation is not about living lifetime after lifetime controlled by karmic debt, but instead is a way to create a new lifetime through free will choices. But why would a soul continue coming back to this planet. The belief that we reincarnate back into this physical reality over-and-over to learn lessons based on our karmic debts, I find shallow and trite. If a soul hasn't learned its karmic debts lifetime after lifetime, then that soul must be incredibly unevolved.

It is my belief we choose the various lifetimes not to learn about karmic debts from previous lifetimes but to experience love and search for new knowledge on a deeper level that assist us on our spiritual journey. We incarnate to gain a deeper expression of love and knowledge so we can have a variety of novel experiences to help us transcend and explore higher states of consciousness as well as exploring a variety of parallel realities. Through the process of transcendence, we become awakened to deeper spiritual knowledge that will guide our journey.

I have pondered reincarnation and karma throughout my life as well as death and the afterlife because my childhood was shaped with those stories. I grew up with a steady diet of tales of haunted houses and other ghost stories told by my maternal grandmother. With this spiritual underpinning, my brother Fred, a funeral director, turned me on to science and began sculpting me for the funeral business when I entered the sixth grade. The funeral business was just another pathway that helped formed my interest in death, the transition of the soul into the afterlife as well as having an innate knowing there were other realities our souls can experience.

By the time I was a sophomore in high school, I knew the procedures of embalming. Unlike most kids my age, I had a very different upbringing. Death and the afterlife were all around me. Not only was I steeped in these influences, but a few years later, I learned from my maternal grandmother, I was born dead. That was a jarring revelation to say the least. Unable to integrate this disclosure, I soon set it aside to get on with my life. However, in the oncoming years, my death at birth, reincarnation and karma became an integral part in understanding death and the afterlife.

The final nail in the coffin (no pun intended) regarding reincarnation and karma was near-death-experiences. I found near-death-experiences eerily similar to my own death experience when I came into this world. I knew there were many after death realities because I had fleeting images from the reality I lived in before I was born. I had insights of being ordered to come to this reality but for what purpose. When I first tried to bring all these concepts together, I had no idea to where they would eventually lead.

I left the funeral business when I was twenty-one years old, deciding to enter the profession of psychology and counseling, and within a decade I was a practicing psychotherapist. I had moved away from death, including my own at birth, so I thought. However, within five years, I was working with people who had AIDS and were dying from that disease. I was back working with death once again. It was at this point I knew I had to integrate whole categories of information and unusual experiences that had peppered my life, including my own death when I was born.

Knowing I came into this world dead has given me insights that there are other realities beyond this material world. Death is not final; there is an afterlife, and this physical reality is not all there is because I had glimpses into some vague other worlds. These ideas and experiences were confirmed with my intense study of science, especially quantum mechanics, specifically the many worlds hypothesis. Science has played a very important role in my life beginning in childhood with a personal chemical lab stocked with chemical and glassware Fred had given me. Years later, to pay for college I took special training in analytic chemistry, which landed me a research position in the chemical industry with a special benefit—they paid for my college education.

While in research chemistry, I discovered the area of quantum mechanics, which brought new insights into the workings of reality. Reality is not what we think it is—it is an illusion. What we think of as material objects is not that at all, but a cloud of potential made manifest physically by our observations creating our reality as well as others. Not only do we create the reality we experience but all sentient beings help to co-create this reality as well as others. We can encounter these realities by altering our consciousness through specific esoteric techniques so we can transcend and experience these realities as well as the afterlife.

The mere fact that we can shift our consciousness to experience a variety of other realities as well as the afterlife realities indicates existence in the physical is impermeant. Everything lives and dies but death is just a transition from one state of being into another or one state of consciousness into another. So, from this perspective death is a shift from our physical being-ness into our spiritual being-ness. Our material bodies die in the physical reality and transitions into the spiritual reality.

But how do we know this is true? Are there ways we can access the beyond while still living in the physical world? Are there methods that can take us into that borderland between life and death as well as other realities? Can we sample the texture of our next spiritual journey? These are valid questions that can only be answered and realized through spiritual techniques and methods.

Death, the afterlife, exploring other realities, my maternal grandmother's pagan spirituality and quantum mechanics were the streams that shaped my interest in magick. From a very early age my maternal grandmother taught me a variety of magickal rituals forming the foundation to study magick and all things esoteric. The magickal stream fit with my religious and spiritual beliefs and endeavors. I knew magick was real because of positive results I got from performing both low and high magick rituals.

Not only was spirituality, religion, magick and science a major part of my life but sexuality was the energetic glue that held the different parts of myself together. Sex has always been the most pleasurable and sacred experience I have had in this uncivilized, violent, and destructive world. I learned early on that sex was sacred because the experience took me into the heights of the most pleasurable experiences by connecting my physical awareness with my soul awareness. I have always felt that religious views surrounding sex especially being gay was created by authorities to control people by stupid laws regarding what sexual acts were deemed okay by the so-called celibate clergy and self-serving lawmakers.

Being gay was unlawful and frowned upon by our hypocritical society that secretly engaged in same sex activity including married men and the clergy. By the time I was seven years old, I knew I was sexually turned on to my gender. When I came to grips with this fact, I eventually became part of the civil rights movement focusing on both racial and sexual injustices.

All five streams—spiritual, religious, magickal, scientific and sexual—laid the foundation for me to become not only a psychotherapist, and a spiritual psychopomp but an Ordained Priest as well. This book is my spiritual journey into the inner awakening of an interconnecting spiritual reality where all things exist in potential. I culled from the world's wisdom traditions and personal discoveries a compilation of methods and techniques that flows gracefully from one into the other exploring my rich spiritual life. These methods and techniques were discovered through personal inner work, ancient esoteric rituals and working with clients as a psychotherapist and spiritual director around dying and death. These procedures led me on a journey of adventure into the vast spiritual landscapes that exist beyond the limited materialistic mentality,

giving meaning and purpose to my life—culminating into becoming an Ordained Priest.

Part One focuses on the turbulent and enlightening years of my youth. It explores my spiritual foundation as well as my religious calling. In those years, I
came to grips with my sexuality both being gay and being sexually abused and
the resulting consequences. Also, I had to deal with my racism living in Jim
Crow South and how that influence propelled me into the civil rights movement. My early career choices are also explored in that I was trained in analytical chemistry opening the door into polymer research. Also, addressed is
the decision to move away from becoming a funeral director into becoming a
psychotherapist with dire consequences from my family.

Part Two focuses on the major spiritual shifts later in my life in which
I began helping people with AIDS go through the dying process and their
accompanying mystical experiences. Also explored are past life experiences,
reincarnation, karma, and near-death experiences. All these experiences laid
the foundation for me to explore the afterlife as well as becoming an Ordained Priest.

Part Three contains the Journey into the Light Imagery used to take
people into the light experience. Also, the Imagery to Connect with the Deceased in the Imaginal Realm, the long and short versions used to communicate with those souls who have crossed over.

Part 1

Turbulent Early Years:
The Good, the Bad and the Ugly

Chapter 1

DEATH BEGAN AT BIRTH

WHEN I WAS A SENIOR IN HIGH SCHOOL, I LEARNED FROM MY MATERNAL grandmother Hattie Turner, I was born dead. Not only was I born dead, but my mother Pauline Turner Duncan did not want me. She was depressed and cried throughout her pregnancy—I was a mistake because the birth control method failed. My mother only wanted two children, so she rejected me from the start, passing me off onto my brother Fred to raise whom was ten years older than I. His influence formed the early blueprint for being a boy by laying a firm foundation in all things masculine. As a result, I bonded with him and never with my mother. With my mother, I always felt I was a burden because she was emotionally cold, distant, controlling, at times physically and verbally abusive, and constantly felt she really didn't love me. Conversely, throughout my early life, I felt my brother Fred was the only person who loved and cared for me—his impact was paramount.

Learning I was born dead and my mother giving me to Fred to raise sent me into a mental and emotional tailspin. Plunged into weeks of intense confusion, I finally began to grasp the impact of how these circumstances shaped my early life. Being estranged from my mother gave me the freedom to explore the world around me in very adventurous ways. I was totally immersed in the world of the masculine except for competitive sports, which I found silly, uninteresting, boring, and brutally competitive. Not only did Fred have an impact on my maleness, but my father Fred Alexander also furthered my male identity by allowing me total access to his vast supply of tools, which I used to build things as well as helping him work on various projects. Although I hardly saw him because he worked second-shift six-days a week as an electro-mechanic in the coalmine, however, he did make time to teach me about tools. He taught me how to respect tools and how to use them safely and to never misuse them because they could be fatal.

Living in the coalmining community of Evarts, Kentucky was fraught with many fears, which influenced my early life. On the days I was not in school, I would watch my father get into his car and drive off to the coalmine, wondering if I would ever see him alive again. The specter of death was always around. I saw neighbors, friends and family members never coming home again because of a mining accident. The fear of my father never coming home haunted my every thought especially when finding out that a neighbor working near him was killed in a mining accident, while my father remained safe.

The awareness of death hung over our entire family and had an extremely negative impact on my mother who was mentally and emotionally unstable. She would sit up late at night until my father made it back home safe. Her fears of death were pervasive and if it hadn't been for my brother Fred, I would have been swallowed up in her melancholic reality. So, being raised by Fred kept my mother's mental and emotional instabilities at a distance, which was a blessing because her influence would have been detrimental.

Although my mother was very unstable, there was one area on which she did have a positive influence and that was my eating habits. She became an organic gardener and began feeding our family healthy foods as well as taking nutritional supplements. The reason she got into natural health was she believed it would cure her mental and emotional problems. However, in the late 1950s and early 1960s, being an organic gardener and taking nutritional supplements was considered by the medical professionals treating her to be a manifestation of her mental illness. Nevertheless, passing along her vast knowledge of natural health was the only constructive gift she gave me, outside of that, she was cold, very shallow, mentally, and emotionally unstable, at times cruel and abusive, and later ended up in a mental hospital.

The other major influence shaping my early spiritual life was my maternal grandmother Hattie Turner who was part Cherokee, Welsh, English and Irish, and like my mother was also emotionally cold. She was a mystic, a spiritual mixture of Cherokee, Celtic/Druid, and pagan Christianity. Her blend of these spiritualities centered on the belief that everything that exists is spirit and everything within the spirit has a soul. She believed the soul was much greater than we think; it is not only the spiritual center within us, but our bodies are embedded within it, and is connected to everything that exists. Being connected to everything means we should respect all creation because everything is alive, exists for specific purposes and is part of ourselves.

Some people considered her a witch because her spirituality included the supernatural, the use of herbs, use of the zodiac signs and natural folk magic, which she did practice. However, within our family she was considered very wise; we would go to her for advice and when we were sick, she would make an herbal remedy and in most cases the remedy worked. She believed all health problems had a spiritual base and could be treated with herbs combined with prayer. These aspects of her spirituality fit perfectly with the stories she would tell in front of the fireplace during the winters and on the front porch during the summers. Her stories laid the foundation for my interest not only in spirituality and natural health, but the supernatural as well, focusing on magic, witchcraft, ghost, and hauntings.

Being an excellent storyteller, she presented her stories in vivid detail by crafting each word with precision. I could see in my mind's eye the story unfolding; I was attached to every word she spoke about the spirit world and knew intuitively there was truth behind those words. With her influence, I realized I had an unusual sense of the spiritual, specifically the afterlife. I knew early on there were unseen populated worlds all around because of fleeting shadowy glimpses into those uncharted domains. It was as though my entrance into this reality was hardwired to live in two worlds—the world of the profane and the world of the spirit.

I believe my grandmother knew I lived in two worlds, because at times she would observe me shifting between the physical world and an unseen imaginal world engaging in conversations with beings I could only experience. I was spiritually different from my brothers as well as from other children and my grandmother knew it. Being spiritually different, she began teaching me specific details about the world of the supernatural, specifically magickal realities. She taught me how to open the veil between this world and the unseen world through magickal spells and rituals. She instructed me how to use and perform various spells and rituals that most people would consider black magick. Years later, I considered these spells to be both white magick and black magick depending on the intention. She stressed intention was how you direct spiritual energy for the spells to work. She did not teach my brothers the spiritual practices she taught me. It was my grandmother who initiated me into the arts of magick, opening the portals into a life of curiosity, enchantment, and wonder.

The first spell she taught me was how to get rid of warts. I was about six years old and had several warts on my hand. She told me to take a piece of salt bacon, go to a crossroad and dig a small hole in the center where the crossroads intersect. Rub the bacon on the warts and bury it in the small hole. After covering the hole with dirt, stand over it, close my eyes and say, "Warts, warts go away, as this bacon rots away." She told me the warts would be gone within week and within that period the warts were gone.

My grandmother's spiritual influence was so pervasive it also had an impact on my brother Fred as well by shaping his interest in how the soul experiences life, death, and the afterlife. Alongside those interests, Fred also had an insatiable appetite for everything related to science, which also rubbed off on me. Later in life Fred was able to bring science together with his interest in life, death, and the afterlife when he became a funeral director. In this regard, these interests helped fuse science with spirituality giving him as well as me a unique perspective. As a result, Fred and my grandmother affected my life deeply, triggering profound insights into the nature of reality both scientifically and spiritually. These insights along with my father's influence on the use of tools and my mother's influence on healthy eating habits marked major transitions in the direction of my life would ultimately take.

The impact my brother had on me regarding science began when I was five years old. Fred had a small chemical and biological laboratory snuggled in a small basement room under our house with a private entrance. One day, he needed help with an experiment and invited me in. This was the first time I had ever been in his lab; I was mystified with all the strange glassware and bottles filled with mysterious powders and liquids. He had me hold a glass container—a beaker with powder in it while he mixed some other chemicals to-gether. He then added the mixture to the powder in the beaker. Suddenly, there was a flash of light and smoke came out of the beaker. Frightened, I dropped the beaker and ran while Fred burst out laughing.

He did not want our parents to know what had happened, so to keep me quiet, he gave me some white powders of my own to experiment with. I have no idea what the powders were, they could have been baking soda and flour for all I knew, but that day marked my interest in science. Science in almost all forms became my passion and Fred continued to fuel that passion by bring-ing me into his lab off and on to help with experiments. Over time, he gave me glassware and more chemicals until I had a small lab of my own. Regarding the chemicals he gave me, the only precautions were to be very careful when adding acids and bases together, and always inspect the labels on chemical bot-tles for skull and crossbones, which meant the contents were poison and could kill me.

The following year when I was six, my parents began buying an old house beside my maternal grandparents' home outside the city limits, overlooking a river at the foot of a mountain that rolled out into a cattle pasture. The cattle pasture was on one side of my grandparents' house and our house was on the other side—we lived in an extended family. Our house was very run down, needed major repairs, and as with most of the houses in the community did not have running water. This meant we used an outside toilet and had to carry water to the main house from an adjacent two-roomed house that had a water line, where my mother washed clothes. We had no indoor plumbing until I was a freshman in high school, and it was only cold water because we had no water heater.

Because there was water in the adjacent two-roomed house, Fred built a larger laboratory for himself in the back room leaving the front room for wash-ing clothes. Once Fred completed furnishing and organizing his lab, he built me a small lab, which was a lab-stand made with shelves attached to a wooden table, taken from a design in a popular science magazine. He stocked my lab-stand with more chemicals and glassware and taught me how to use them safely. At that age, I played most childhood games—all the while experiment-ing with my chemicals, creating exciting new substances, and watching intri-guing chemical reactions.

Not only did Fred shape my interest in science but he also taught me how to dance. He was sixteen, dating and needed a dance partner to learn the jitterbug, so at six years old, I became his default dance partner. He swirled me around and floated me over his shoulders as he refined his dance moves all with the intention of enticing his dates. Although I was content with my childhood play, learning to dance added a new dimension to my life that would last for years. Unbeknownst to what was waiting for me on the horizon, my experiences were heading toward radical changes, opening new vistas in science, spirituality, sexuality, and racism.

Shortly after moving into our dilapidated house, two incidents occurred that shook my childhood world. The first event was my parents took me to my paternal step-grandfather's vigil. Although I knew about death from mining accidents, this was my first vigil experience. As it turned out, it was a large affair at his home with copious amounts of food and drink as well as tears and laughter. With sandwich in hand, I found myself at his casket. Over the viewing portion of the casket was a veil made of mesh cloth to keep out insects. I stared at the body for a while, then slid my hand under the veil and touched his hand. It was stone cold. I jerked my hand back as quickly as possible.

At the time, the experience was very perplexing; I simply could not grasp why he was so cold and where his life went. Although there was no life in his body, something didn't seem right. I had an odd feeling; he appeared to be gone, but I knew on some level he wasn't. People kept telling me he had gone to heaven. But where was heaven? I was confused! Nothing they said felt right or made sense.

My confusion only deepened with the second incident. I was sitting in our living room one evening shortly after we moved, listening to my maternal grandmother's storytelling, when we saw a fire blazing through the window. We went outside, stood on the porch watching a fire raging across the river at the foot of a mountain not far from where we use to live. As the fire blazed it became obvious what was burning—a cross. We all stood paralyzed, transfixed at the eerie burning cross—I couldn't take my eyes off it, and it was very ominous and unsettling.

After the cross burned, I asked my grandmother what just happened. She said, "That was for bad women." Still puzzled, she continued telling me that they (whoever they were) put a bundle of switches on bad women's porches and if they didn't change their ways, they burned a cross. If the bad women didn't change after the cross was burned, they ran them out of town. I was still confused because I didn't understand what bad women were and what the cross burning really meant. It was many years later that I finally learned the cross burning was a KKK activity to terrorize black people. Living in the South, I guess the reason my grandmother lied to me was because she wanted to protect me from the truth. I can honestly say, I was terrorized by that event, and it has never left my memory.

A year after my step-grandfather's death and the cross burning, which was laden with confusion, another unusual experience rocked my childhood when I got my first dog. I named him Laddy, and he became my constant companion; we went everywhere together. One sunny day when I was seven, Laddy and I took a long hike in the mountains above our house. We were following cow paths that meandered through the dense grass and trees. I could tell cattle had been there earlier because some of the grass had been trampled and eaten, and there were no spider-webs crossing the pathways, which were always present.

We came to a wide clearing near an old, abandoned coalmine. The clearing was encircled with tall trees and grass, the perfect spot to rest and eat. The sun was beaming down through an opening in the tall trees, as a gentle breeze slightly moved the grass and tree leaves. I took off my backpack and canteen of water. Laddy and I sat down soaking in the warm sunshine.

I took out of the backpack two potted meat sandwiches my mother had packed earlier. I gave Laddy one of the sandwiches and ate the other. As we ate, I could hear the trees rustling as the breeze picked up speed. The sounds of birds surrounded us, as well as the echoing sounds of water coming out of the nearby abandoned coalmine. Over time the stream of water formed a small brook that ran down the mountainside into the river below.

After eating, Laddy and I ran freely through the tall grass feeling the warm summer breeze caressing my skinny, suntanned body. Looking up through a large opening in the canopy of trees at the sunny blue sky, I noticed there was not a cloud to be seen. I felt very comfortable and deeply connected with my friend Laddy, as we ran and played. I would run ahead of him and whistle then he would pick up speed and run ahead of me.

Suddenly the warmth of the sun felt different, everything around me seemed to change—I stopped running. I stood frozen on the path as feelings came over me that were different from anything I had experienced before. It felt as though my body was light as a feather. I began feeling strange sensations of being lifted up, suspended in mid-air and could float from tree limb to tree limb with ease. Although I had those sensations, I knew on some level, I was still planted firmly on the ground.

Then the breeze stopped and there was stillness. Feelings engulfed me as though I was in a vacuum. Everything suddenly became still and silent, and there was no fear of what was happening. Out of my periphery, Laddy lay down in a comfortable curl.

My perception abruptly changed, noticing everything was getting brighter. The trees, the grass, the blue sky appeared different, and every color became more vivid and vibrant, as though I could see energy patterns of all the various shapes and shades of nature. These energy patterns appeared to connect one part of nature to another.

Then in this suspended stillness, there were feelings of being protected and loved, as I floated in a profound sea of calmness. It was a peaceful feeling of total acceptance with no conditions, nothing I had felt before. I also had a strange sensation, I was connected to everything, and everything was connected to me—a feeling of profound oneness. Then as quickly as it came, it was over, and I was back in everyday reality but confused. Laddy began jumping on me and wagging his tail. Although confused, I was not frightened because there was a feeling I was not alone, an inner presence—something was with me that had not been there before.

Walking back home, I desperately tried to forget what had just happened, but couldn't. I walked over to a large rock that jetted out beside the pigpen where I often played with my friends. Sat down on the rock and stared aimlessly at the cattle pasture alongside my grandparents' home. Suddenly, I was shaken out of my reverie when hearing my neighbor telling his dogs to get out of the way, so he could feed the chickens.

Years later, I discovered this was an experience of rapture. The experience was so profound that when I was in the woods or alongside the river, I always had feelings of being connected with everything. As time went on, these feelings became so pervasive and integrated within me that when I was alone, whether in the woods or along the river, I would feel that deep interconnectedness as well as that inner peaceful presence.

A few weeks later, still trying to push the rapture experience out of my mind, another experience rocked my world. My brother Fred, now in the Army, came home on furlough. He gave me two books and with a smile and a nod told me they were about our family's religion. One of the books was a New Testament and the other was a Roman Catholic Missal (mass book). I didn't know how serious he was, but at my young age, I took what he said to heart. I now had something I had not had before a religious identity; I was Roman Catholic. I devoured the pictures in the two books and later learned to read the words. However, up until that time, I had no religion, except for the pagan spirituality my maternal grandmother had taught me, which was not Roman Catholic. I learned about Jesus not from my maternal grandmother or other family members, but from the Christian missionaries that came to our school.

These Christian missionaries had a major impact on me. They taught me all about Jesus as they demonstrated his life story on a flannel board replete with cloth picture cutouts. The missionaries came several times a year and totally indoctrinated me into the Christian religion. I was indoctrinated from age six to around eleven when the missionaries were prohibited from continuing their Christian indoctrination because the Constitution forbid it. By that time, I was totally programmed to believe Jesus was a real person and I knew for certain he existed. With this influence, I later took up the mission to find more facts regarding the historic Jesus.

Years later, I learned Fred was joking about our family being Roman Catholic, but nonetheless, I now had a Christian identity. As I was accepting my religious identity as a Roman Catholic, there was a shift in my behavior. It was as though some unknown force was directing me to become a priest. Was it the presence inside, I did not know. When pets died, I would make them a casket and bury them alongside the mountain stream fed by the water coming from the old, abandoned coalmine. I used verses from the New Testament and the Roman Catholic Missal to perform funerals. I even included headstones creating a small pet cemetery alongside the stream, setting the stage for what was to come.

On the heels of dealing with my oneness experience and accepting my religious identity, I had an unusual dream or what I thought was a dream. In the dream, I was lying with my hands behind my head with interlocking fingers on the arched hillside cattle pasture alongside my grandparents' home. I was looking up at the moonless night sky at the bright stars dotting the black background. Looking out of my eyes, I could see I was wearing a red plaid flannel shirt, blue jeans and cowboy boots my oldest brother Orville (a.k.a. Lee) had given me after he married.

Looking at the bright stars, I noticed several began to move. Not only did they move, but they also began to descend toward me and took on a bluish coloration. I became aware they were not stars at all, but five angular box-like structures. They were huge and the bluish coloration were bright blue lights all over the angular structures. The objects were breathtakingly beautiful. There was no fear at all, only a secure feeling of warmth. Suddenly the objects began to ascend back into the black heavenly background and became stars again.

From that time onward, this dream would reoccur, but there was a difference. Rather than looking up at the night sky, I became the observer watching myself looking up at the night sky. In these subsequent dreams, I was waiting for something to happen, for the objects to return, but they never did. The feelings I had in those recurring dreams were feelings of deep longing, but a longing for what?

It was as though my seventh year of life was laying the foundation for the person I would ultimately become. The final awakening charted a path of no return—my sexuality. Up until that time, all my sexual fantasies were heterosexual, although my sexual experiences were with both male and female friends. At the time, I only had sexual fantasies and did not masturbate, however, that was about to change with my cousin Robert (pseudonym) who taught me how to masturbate in an outhouse at my paternal step-grandfather's vigil. Robert and I continued to experience each other sexually until he joined the Army many years later. The sexual experiences with Robert were not my first sexual encounters. According to Fred, when I was almost four, he caught a neighbor boy, two years older than I, performing oral sex on me. This was most likely my first sexual encounter and a few years later, sex was always present and very enjoyable with most of my male friends.

With girls however, it was just taking off our clothes, touching each other and inspecting each other's bodies giving me details of what girls looked like. My perception of females was also enriched with my sister-in-law Irma, my brother Orville's first wife. Shortly after Orville and Irma married, they had to move in with us because of lack of money. They slept in the bed next to mine, and it wasn't long before Irma began changing clothes in front of me. Because I was a child, she probably didn't think anything about it.

From the start, Irma and I had a unique relationship beginning when Orville first started dating her. Unlike my mother and grandmother who were emotionally cold, Irma was warm and engaging. She doted on me constantly, making me feel very special and giving me small gifts—I loved being around her. They finally found an apartment and moved out of the house. Once settled, Orville started college and was away through the week and home on weekends, which created major martial problems. Throughout this period, I hardly saw Irma or Orville and had no idea what was going on between them. I missed Irma deeply.

There was a Christmas parade coming to town, and my parents told me we would see Orville and Irma at the parade. I couldn't wait to see her, being the first female in my life that cared about me. As we stood watching the floats go by, my attention was looking for Irma. I finally saw her down the street walking toward us. With a rush of excitement, I ran toward her with arms outstretched and within a few feet she said in a condescending angry tone, "Get out of my face, you little brat!" I froze in my tracks, stunned—I couldn't move—I was shattered. The first female I ever had a positive connection with had left me feeling abandoned, rejected and heart broken. This event would have a lasting impact on me regarding women—I simply couldn't trust them with my emotions.

Although Irma had rejected me, she still gave me a detailed view of what a mature woman looked like physically, a stark contrast from what I saw with little girls. However, I cobbled together these two views of females and created a fantasy of a Marilyn Monroe picture I had seen. Marilyn became the centerpiece of all my fantasies. These fantasies were just images of Marilyn's nude body and nothing else.

One day, while fantasizing about Marilyn an unexpected person dropped into my fantasy—Paul, a classmate. In the fantasy, I had to choose who would be my sexual partner Marilyn or Paul. I chose Paul, which awakened me to my sexual orientation. From that moment on, I knew I was turned on to my gender. I no longer entertained sex with Marilyn Monroe, or any woman. This became one of my hidden secrets and I simply did not know what to do with it.

After the experiences at my step-grandfather's vigil, the cross burning and the other four experiences when I was seven, I began having thoughts and feelings I was different. I no longer fit in with the world around me, feeling out of place, feeling I'm not from here, feeling unusual, and feeling I was not anchored to this reality. Moreover, I knew I was living in two worlds at once, the world of the physical and the world on the spiritual. I had a deep knowing I'm only passing through this physical reality—this is not my true home, I'm from somewhere else.

These thoughts and feelings continued in various combinations throughout my life. In the years to come, I would focus on the fact I was born dead and not wanted by my mother, at other times I focused on awakening to my sexuality, which only added to my perceptions of alienation and being different. I was also being flooded with a plethora of unusual feelings connected with strange images and insights triggering profound questions. I questioned was my family really my family; how I could have been born into this family because I was so different.

As the years unfolded, the feeling of oneness, the awareness of an inner presence, the after-effects of the unusual dream, and of course my sexuality, all haunting my every thought. I wondered was the inner presence something that came into me from the reality I lived in before I was born or was it a part of me that suddenly awakened. Was the inner presence the unknown force that was guiding me to become a priest, and why did I have an intense longing to go back to somewhere else, but where? Why did I know my step-grandfather was not really dead, but existed somewhere else?

Chapter 2
DESCENDING INTO MADNESS

MY MOTHER'S PREGNANCY WITH ME WAS VERY DETRIMENTAL, SETTING the stage for a descent into madness. She simply didn't want any more children; I was a mistake and felt that all through my life. My brother Fred whom I felt was the only one who truly loved me was forced into the position of being my parent. My mother just did not want to deal with me; I was a burden and we never bonded. From my birth onward, my mother began living in a fantasy world she created to protect her from all inconveniences. I later learned she became childlike throughout that period and had problems coping with the simplest of problems.

Her fantasy world was shaken when she discovered my brother Orville was dating a woman named Irma and intended to marry her. Unbeknownst to Orville, Irma had the reputation of being a very loose woman. Everyone in town knew she was sexually loose except Orville, and this was the pivotal trigger sending my mother further into mental and emotional instability. My father later told me, the day my mother found out Orville was going to marry Irma she was in the kitchen chewing gum. Upon hearing about the marriage, she suddenly went into a daze and began chewing the gum faster and faster almost in a panic—my mother never accepted the marriage.

She suddenly began to drastically change our eating habits and as if overnight the bacon grease container disappeared from the kitchen stove. She went through strange eating behaviors from eating pig brains with eggs to rejecting almost all meats, all the while occupying her time with organic gardening. She loaded up on vitamins and nutritional supplements, only read literature on organic gardening and natural health, and years later became a vegetarian. She thought this would help her mental and emotional problems.

Alongside my mother dealing with Orville's marriage to Irma, her father my grandfather Robert Turner was becoming gravely ill. His health continued to deteriorate from 1957 to January 1960 when he finally died, sending my mother further into madness. However, throughout this period there were changes taking place in my life as well. There was a major shift away from Fred raising me because he had married his teenage sweetheart Delilah and moved to Chicago to enter mortuary school. During this period, my mother tried to step up to her responsibilities as a mother but with very little success, so my maternal grandmother began sharing in the responsibility of raising me. My mother continued to abdicate almost all her responsibilities as a mother and a wife.

She was totally consumed with my grandfather's illness, to the point, I was left on my own to raise myself. My grandmother tried to give me some guidance, but she became preoccupied with helping my mother. At ten years of age, I felt abandoned, lost, fearful, unsure and was looking for some parental attention and guidance, but there was none. However, a female neighbor began to take up the slack by giving me attention, which was what I was craving. The neighbor knew I loved to eat cornbread and mulberry jelly, made fresh from the mulberry tree that joined out properties.

She enticed me into her house one day to eat some cornbread and mulberry jelly, she had just made. As I munched on the delicious treat, she guided me through her house and we ended up in her bedroom. The next thing I knew, she had trapped me in a corner of her bedroom and held me there while she took off her clothes and forced me to fondle her breast and crotch. The smell was horrific—unlike any smell I had encountered and is hard to describe. I just couldn't get the smell out of my mind, and it is still in my olfactory memory to this day.

As I fondled her, she pulled my face into her breast, and I began to feel her hand almost touching my crotch as I was trying to wiggle free. I pulled back, seeing her eyes were closed; at that moment, she moved to one side forming an opening to escape. I pulled away from her and ran quickly, darting for the front door and to safety. My neighbor tried a second time to entice me into her home with the same treat; I didn't take the bait and was never in her house again.

This was a strange period, with my mother spinning out of control and my grandmother trying to comfort her, I had no one to tell what had happened, I kept the secret hidden. As I was trying to come to some resolution over being sexually assaulted, I found myself reading more. Reading became my only friend allowing me to escape from the trauma. I first read adventure novels such as *Treasure Island* but slowly shifted to science and religion. And if trying to escape from being sexually molested wasn't enough, I found myself suddenly dealing with a new problem. Without warning, my mother began listening to a fundamentalist hell-fire preacher on the radio. Through his influence, she began telling me I was doomed to hell because of sin. Hell was a new concept for me and at first couldn't grasp what it meant. I had heard the term used many times before in the context of cursing, but it was my mother that added the gruesome details. She told me there was no hope for me because the devil had his grips on my soul. I was lost forever in sin and will live eternally in the fires of hell and would never get out. I became terrified with what she was saying!

Also, during this period listening to the radio preacher, my mother became physically abusive. With small transgressions that never garnered a spanking, things now had changed. In one sermon, the radio preacher said that to keep a child from going to hell, never spare the rod. My mother went from spanking me with switches for minor infractions to using a stick of splintery kindling to beat me. She would beat the devil out of me, so I could go to heaven to meet Jesus. As my mother went through her abusive tirades, my grandmother was just watching the whole affair looking helpless.

As my grandfather's health continued to deteriorate, my mother's accusations of me going to hell increased with more beatings. Then a couple of months after turning eleven, my grandfather finally died, and my mother totally lost it mentally. Her beatings and accusations of me being a sinner abruptly stopped, and she just sat with a dazed look on her face. At that point, my grandmother immediately moved into our home to raise me. The next thing I knew, my mother had totally disappeared. I was later informed by both my grandmother and father that she was in a hospital.

☆☆☆

Although my mother was gone, I really didn't miss her because my grand-mother was already raising me and now was living with us. I felt very relieved of not being beat and told I was a sinner going to hell. I was finally told my mother was in St. Albans Hospital in Radford, Virginia and later discovered it was a private mental hospital. After three months of no mother, my father told me and my grandmother, we were going to take a trip to the hospital to visit her.

Since I was under the age of twelve, the hospital rules were I could not visit my mother; so I would sit in the waiting room waiting for my father and grandmother to conclude their visits. During our stay in Radford, my grand-mother and father visited the hospital several times, while the nurse on evening duty got to know me sitting in the waiting room. On the last visit, the nurse asked if I would like to see my mother, and with cautious excitement, I said, "Yes." What I remember, she took out a set of keys, guided me to a large wooden door and unlocked it. We entered a very small room with a metal door; she unlocked the metal door, and we entered another small room with a barred door. She unlocked the barred door, and we entered a large room with many people meandering around.

I stood looking at all the people and asked where my mother was. The nurse pointed toward a spinning wheel beside a fireplace and told me she was sitting in the chair next to it, with my father and grandmother. She guided me over to where my mother was. I just stood there for a moment and then touched her shoulder. She turned and looked up at me with glazed eyes and said, "Who are you?"

Startled, I stared at her for a moment and said, "Gary."

She then replied, "Who's Gary?"

I stood frozen, shaking in my shoes, unable to speak and totally confused, my mother didn't know who I was. That moment on some level I knew my mother had died. Our relationship had never been great, but now it would never be the same; it had ended at a time when I was dealing with being sex-ually abused. Now without a mother who had verbally and physically abused me, I felt a deep confusing emptiness. My father realized he could not be an adequate parent working second-shift in the coalmines, so to remedy the problem, he completely gave that responsibility over to my grandmother. It was now her duty to raise me.

The strain on my grandmother raising me was very severe. I had no idea how bad things were when one day, I heard her talking to herself. I was just waking up from the night's sleep and heard her talking to herself in the adjacent room. At first, I couldn't accept what I thought I heard, but she repeated it again. She was disgusted with the situation of having to raise me. She said mumbling to herself, "I've already raised a family and resent having to raise another one!" She hated the situation she was now in and resented me. I felt further abandoned, alone and simply unwanted. Every woman in my life had abandoned me. My life would never be the same.

My mother was finally released from the mental hospital after many months and twelve electro-convulsive shock treatments. Over time, she became addicted to what she called "nerve pills" rendering her aloof, in a constant fog and staring into nowhere. However, she continued her organic food and vitamin supplement obsession. The beatings had stopped for a while then slowly began again, ending when I was in the eighth grade. One day for a minor infraction, she took a wooden stick and started to beat me; I swiftly grabbed her wrist and stopped her. Startled, she backed off because I now stood a little taller and was stronger than she. This was the last time she tried to physically abuse me because I could now fight back.

As a result of being both physically and sexually abused, it now seemed I was a target for adults to touch me inappropriately. On the heels of being molested by my female neighbor, the man who owned the grocery where we shopped began touching my ass—teasingly. I would move away from him, and he would give me a small bottle of Coca Cola and continue touching my ass in front of my father who just laughed at the so-called play. I didn't like it but felt my father approved; I was trapped, feeling helpless and could do nothing.

After my mother was out of the mental hospital, she no longer listened to the radio preacher, but started attending a fundamentalist church introduced to her by my sister-in-law Delilah. This was the church her family attended and was the first church my mother dragged me to; I was in the sixth grade and detested it. I felt out of place, did not like the people and it was very different from what I knew about the Roman Catholic Church I embraced.

It wasn't long before I was sexually accosted in this church. Leaving the church after service, the choir director would give me a tight friendly hug at the door, as his hand slowly moved from my shoulders down my back to my ass as he continued to hold me close to his body as he massaged my butt cheeks. I was confused, lost, feeling totally prayed-upon, and trapped—I had nowhere to turn—I was now a sexual target.

These sexual abusive encounters were very puzzling because the pastor of the church, Revered S., constantly preached about the evil sins of sex. If sex was so evil, then why was the choir director playing with my ass every chance he got. And to top it off, this so-called preacher, preaching the evil sins of sex, had an affair with the church pianist who was in her late teens. Not only was he in this clandestine affair, but he got her pregnant, which resulted in a secret illegal abortion, which was gossiped about in the church. All was kept secret until the pianist's family confronted the preacher, who by the way was married and had two children. As you can guess he quickly left the church and disappeared—an abrupt ending to a fatal hypocrite.

If sex was so evil, then why did it feel so good. At my age, I could not understand the problem with sex because my friends and I were having sex all the time especially with my cousin Robert. As long as I was having sex with my peers everything was okay, but with adults it felt unclean and dirty as well as feeling dominated and controlled. I simply didn't like adults touching me sexually. However, with my friends sex was beautiful, bonding, pleasurable and simply delightful and not the evil sin I was told it was. I was becoming aware there was something wrong with what I was being told about sex but at the time couldn't figure it out.

It seemed the world around me had become extremely uncertain and confusing as I found myself introduced into more madness. The month before I entered the seventh grade, we took a trip to Union, South Carolina to visit relatives on my maternal grandmother's side of the family. It had been about a year since my mother had been released from St. Albans Hospital, and my father and grandmother thought the trip would be good for my mother's mental condition. I was feeling more disconnected from my family, alienated, unsure, unwanted, and just tolerated. I kept a low profile, keeping out of their way, rafting on the river, hiking, sex play with friends and experimenting with my chemicals.

The trip to Union, South Carolina was long and hot because we had no air conditioner and the interstate highway systems had not been completed at the time. This would be the trip in which I learned the deplorable secrets of my relatives. I was aware enough to know there were racial differences and tensions between whites and blacks growing up in the South. However, living in the coalmining community, whites and blacks lived together and under the same fear of losing loved ones and friends to mining accidents. When disaster struck, there were no blacks and whites because most of the community came together to help; this was evident when I was four years old. An African American family named Drummond that lived up and across the road from us had a disaster on a Christmas Eve. Their house caught fire and burned to the ground losing their grandmother, daughter, and an unborn baby to the fire. Most of the community came together to help the family including my family.

One day after the fire, our family was in the kitchen and my mother was talking about the Drummond family and described the gruesome details of the fire. The fire started in the kitchen while the pregnant daughter was asleep, and smoke overtook her. Being unconscious, the intense fire began burning her body. As she was burning her lower abdomen burst open and the baby popped out only to be partially consumed by the flames. Although I was four, I could see in my mind the baby popping out, I was sickened!

During this time, black and white kids could play army together, could swim together in the same river swimming hole, but certain areas remained off limits such as Jim Crow's separate restroom, seating in the movie theater, and going to separate schools and churches. Some mornings, my black playmates and I would walk to school together; they would go to their school, and I would go to mine. I did notice they were using books we no longer used because they were outdated. At the time, I had not thought too much about race; things were the way they were, and I didn't question. But this trip changed all that.

Race was not talked about in our house; my father accepted everyone. However, on this trip to South Carolina, I became aware for the first time of racial tensions. Listening to the grown-ups in the southern muggy night air talk about race was something totally new to me. I would hear them laugh and squawk about racial issues, especially integration. I soon learned the meaning of the cross burning I had witnessed when I was six. I also learned that some of my relatives in the small town of Union were members of the KKK. My relatives talked openly about burning crosses, lynching black men that were after white women. As this talk went on, I noticed my father, mother and grandmother did not participate, but only nodded with forced smiles. I had never been exposed to the blatant racism I was now experiencing.

The adults thought I needed to see the town and to be with boys, so I was taken to a distant cousin several years older than I who would show me around. As family members were getting reacquainted, my cousin told me to get in his car and off we went. Within about fifteen minutes, he had picked up a friend, who would accompany my cousin in showing me around. On separate occasions, cruising around town, I noticed the language in the car shifted. The conversation turned to, "Them damn niggers and Jews." My cousin's friend was now doing most of the driving. He stopped the car, turned to me in the back seat and asked, "What's the different between a nigger and a Jew?"

I said I didn't know. He laughed and said, "There ain't no difference. One's black and one's white, they're both niggers," and laughed.

He then looked me straight in the eyes and said, "You think I hate niggers don't you. Well, I don't. I think every white man should own one." He and my cousin burst out laughing.

The last night I was with my cousin and his friend turned to abject terror. Out of nowhere, they asked how much money my father was worth. I told them I didn't know, but they kept asking me over and over. As my cousin's friend drove, we entered a forest area I had not seen before. My cousin's friend said, "Your daddy has to have money to pay us because we're going to kidnap you!" They both burst out laughing as terror engulfed me. I began shivering all over, trembling from my head to my feet. I don't know who said it, but I heard, "Your daddy has to pay." Between them, they discussed where to hide me and asked again about my father's worth. I finally told them my father was a coalminer and didn't know how much he was worth. Then there was a shift:

"Well then let's take him back." Silence permeated the car; as they finally pulled up in front of my relative's home, I opened the car door and ran as fast as I could hearing them laughing.

Being in a state of confusion, feeling not wanted, uncertain and needing adult guidance, I was ripe for racist indoctrination. That trip to Union, South Carolina left me in a state of terror as well as pumped full of racism. I was now persuaded that black people were my enemy and needed to be feared and hated along with Jews, because they were going to integrate our schools and take over the country. The odd thing, I didn't know what a Jew was. I had never met anyone Jewish, and I was supposed to hate them. I later discovered most of my family were racist and had done many cruel things to black people, especially black men going back to the late 1800s.

Chapter 3
Following in My Brother's Footsteps

Officiating pet funerals and burying them was a prelude for things to come with my brother Fred. He and I had a very close relationship not only because he introduced me into the world of science, but also because the first seven years of my life, he was instrumental in raising me. He was the only one in my family I felt loved me, and his influence was instrumental in helping shape the direction my life would take. By the fifth grade, I finally realized Fred was in mortuary school studying to be a funeral director. Because of my experiences at my paternal step-grandfather's vigil and burying pets, I now had an idea what he was studying.

While studying mortuary science, Fred made a calculated decision that would deepen my interest in science, religion, and spirituality. When I was between the ages of eleven and twelve, Fred slowly began giving me his laboratory. I quickly combined it with what I already had and dove deeper into chemistry, biology, and astronomy—I was ecstatic. However, Fred had an ulterior motive with this move; he was sculpting me to follow in his footsteps. This became clear during the Christmas holiday when he gave me two plastic models to assemble, the visible man and visible woman. Putting the models together and painting the organs gave me a basic understanding of human anatomy. This was reinforced when he and Delilah visited later that year. Fred would quiz me about anatomy, biology, and chemistry, and on that visit gave me a college textbook on human physiology. From the text, he began teaching me how the human body worked.

In our family, many interesting conversations occurred at the kitchen table and on that visit, an interesting discussion took place regarding science and religion. As I sat silently listening to Fred talk about science, religion, and God, I noticed my mother was becoming agitated at what he was saying, which was in opposition to her religious beliefs. Fred indicated he thought God was a group of higher scientific beings that created us in a laboratory. Just like we create various strains of microorganisms and look through a microscope to manipulate them. He stressed these higher scientific beings are doing the same things to us as we do to microorganisms. They created our world and all things in it, and just like what we do with bacteria, they look through their microscopes at their creations, which is us.

As Fred talked, I could envision what he was saying because he had given me a microscope and I had looked at bacteria and protozoa that I had grown in my lab. I thought what he said made sense. This metaphor gave me insight into beings higher than myself that were scientist and not the Christian god the missionaries had taught me in elementary school. At the time, I did not connect it with the presence inside me, but with his explanation, I had a broader view of both physical and spiritual reality. I began to reason we were created by unseen higher scientific beings that watch and manipulate us. This reasoning stayed with me throughout my life because I would often wonder what these beings were like and how did they create the universe around me.

The following summer before the eighth grade, my maternal grandmother and I visited Fred and Delilah in Chicago. During the visit, he began teaching me cultural burial rituals, more anatomy and physiology, and introduced the topics of embalming theory and practice, and embalming chemistry. By the time school started, my scientific horizons had expanded to include mortuary science. However, the school year brought an unsuspected awakening not only into a new field of science, but an awareness of a deeper level of spirituality.

Every spring where we lived, the valley below would flood, and this year was no different. It had rained relentlessly for three days with severe flooding and schools was cancelled. On the fourth day the rain stopped, and my cousin

Robert came to our house with a friend of ours, Tom, to persuade me to play a game of army. They brought their toy rifles and were ready for a game. I hadn't played army since the sixth grade and wasn't interested in playing at all, but after much persuasion, I gave in. After finding my old toy rifle that had been stored, we chose sides and as usual I was the lone enemy. I took off in the mountains to hide and hid behind a tree waiting for my cousin and Tom to find me.

Peering from behind a tree, I saw them in the distance searching for me. As I watched, it dawned on me that if the rifle I was holding was real, I could pick them off easily. For the first time in my life, I became deeply aware of what a soldier was and what army was all about. It was about killing people. In the pit of my stomach, I had a sickening feeling; I didn't want to have anything to do with killing people. Although I honored my uncles who fought in the European and Pacific theaters during World War II, I also honored my father who build ships in Baltimore for the war effort, but I realized at that moment, I didn't want anything to do with the military killing machine and still feel that way to this day.

Not only was I sickened with the idea of killing people, but I was emotionally moving in a very different spiritual direction, one of non-violence. I was also entering a new phase in my sexuality rather than just having sex as I was having with my cousin, I was now forming deeper emotional relationships. At the time, I had two special friends Tim and Larry with whom I had deep emotional connections. Tim was the son of the preacher who took over the church after Reverend S left; the church my mother forced me to attend. Tim and I would get together every Sunday from the seventh grade and throughout the eighth grade and developed a deep emotional bond with each other. Our affections were simply holding and caressing each other, and over time eventually led to sex.

With Larry the situation was very different. Shortly after becoming friends in the eighth grade, Larry wanted to have sex with me, which surprised me. Because I had a relationship with Tim, it took some time before Larry convinced me to have sex with him, and when it finally happened, we formed an emotional bond enjoying the sacred connection.

At first, my feelings for Larry were not the same as I had for Tim, but over time our affections grew, and he became my special friend. This mainly happened after Tim left the area because his father was no longer the pastor of the church. Larry and I were sexually and emotionally involved until we were sophomores in high school and had to stop our special relationship because we were socially pressured to get girlfriends. It was peer pressure that created much confusion and disgust toward the cultural mores forcing me to date. I did not feel comfortable with girls because with my history I could not trust them and did not find them interesting but played along with the dating game. With girls, what bothered me the most was all they talked about was getting married and having babies something I definitely did not want. My sexual interest was now completely with my own gender; I only dated girls because of social pressure.

I soon discovered after playing army with Robert and Tom, I no longer wanted to harm people and now had a deep emotional connection to helping people in need. I also realized that helping people could be achieved through discoveries in science and medicine, and that was the career path I needed to take. In this respect, I felt working in my lab and later in other labs would eventually lead to new medicines to help fight diseases and relieve pain and suffering I saw all around me.

However, as I was entertaining a career in medical science, there was a shift taking place in my scientific interest, which now included a new area— physics. I discovered physics was at the forefront of time travel, an interest I had for some time. I realized if I could time travel, I could leave the present world, which I didn't like for a better future world, one not fraught with killing, pain and suffering that I witnessed all around me daily. I simply did not like the reality I was in and wanted to find a way out!

Like Fred, my eighth grade science teacher Margaret Smith had a huge impact in sculpting the direction my science career would take. Besides my maternal grandmother, Margaret was one of the few women that had a positive impact on me, she with science and my grandmother with spirituality. At the time, I was strong in science and weak in math, but that would soon change. Although at first I was leery of Margaret, within a few weeks into the eighth grade, she discovered my deep interest and knowledge in science, especially chemistry. Moreover, what accelerated my scientific interest was a weekly classroom science magazine that began helping to refine my interest in physics. The science magazine coupled with two books captured my imagination, H. G. Wells' *The Time Machine* and Martin Gardner's *Relativity for the Million*. Although I accelerated in all areas of science, Gardner's book turned me on to math. What was disappointing was I could only read Gardner's book and study it during class-time because the book belonged to the science class and couldn't be loaned out.

In Gardner's book, one formula broadened my interest in math, the Lorentz-FitzGerald contraction or transformation formula that sent me on a quest to build a time machine. I knew if I could build a time machine using the information in this formula, I would move forward in time and experience the future as Wells described, but without the human eating Morlocks. I also felt I could find out where I was really from in reference to the dream I had when I was seven—was I from a future world or another planet or some other reality.

After working through the mechanics of building a time machine, I presented my idea to the science class and Margaret was very encouraging and supportive. I used the Lorentz-FitzGerald formula to support my argument. I knew if I could build a contraption that could spin close to the speed of light that would propel me into the future. A machine I did build, but using a washing machine motor; my heavy contraption did not budge, although it did blow several fuses. Even though my contraption did not work, I knew I was on the right track, but needed to study Gardener's book more in depth. I finally saved enough money to purchase Gardner's book for my very own and I still have it to this day.

Although I was immersed in science and dealing with my sexuality, racism was still at the forefront. By the end of the eighth grade, we were informed that the next year, our school would be integrated. I decided to drop out of school rather than face the violence that surely would happen as prophesied by my

South Carolina relatives. When I told my mother I wasn't going back to school because of integration, she asked the wisest question, which was very unusual for her. She said, "Gary Wayne, who do you play and go swimming with?" I named a few white friends and then said, "Pepper" a black playmate. I quickly understood my life was already partially integrated. In addition, Pepper and I had had several sexual experiences when I was in the sixth grade before my relatives in South Carolina had indoctrinated me into racism. However, I still knew I had to brace myself for the oncoming violence. My freshman year was integrated without a hitch—very peaceful, contrary to what my relatives had forced down my throat.

Not only had I experienced a smooth integration, but I began moving away from my mother's church by refusing to attend. Religiously, I was in a fog because I knew I was Roman Catholic and disliked my mother's church with a passion. I saw the members of her church as being very ignorant. By the time I was entering my sophomore year, a few Catholics had entered my life and one was a mixed blessing, James Otis.

I became acquainted with James Otis years before I was twelve; he was the uncle to my good friend Tom. When I first saw James Otis, I was a small child trading comic books with Tom. Around the age of twelve, I began visiting Tom at his home to play games, which eventually turned to chess. James Otis's interactions with me changed drastically. He began giving me something I seldom had—compliments—especially on my hair. By the time I was thirteen, James Otis began running his fingers through my hair and over time he began giving me small gifts. As with a lot of older men, he became very touchy and by the time I was a freshman in high school the touches eventually ended up in my crotch accompanied with small amounts of money. Every time he fondled me, he gave me a dollar; this eventually led me into the world of prostitution and pornography.

Even though, I had to deal with the sexual aspects of the relationship with James Otis, which we kept very secret, there was another aspect that was very positive—the Roman Catholic religion—James Otis was Catholic. I began learning a lot about the Roman Catholic religion through him and got turned on to the Trappist Monk Thomas Merton. Through Merton's writings, I began dealing with my racism; his impact gave me the strength to confront my racist attitudes. Although James Otis turned me on to Thomas Merton, he was an ardent racist and hated almost anyone who wasn't white. These same racist attitudes, I found later that year with my brother Fred who I discovered was also an ardent racist.

With James Otis' influence, I internalized everything Catholic, began dealing with my homosexuality and through Thomas Merton's writing began letting go of my racist attitudes. However, racism slowly began raising its ugly head once again with Fred. Fred had graduated from mortuary school, which drained his finances. He and Delilah decided to leave Chicago and move back to Kentucky where things were less expensive so they could save money. He decided to work in several funeral homes getting more apprenticeship training and increasing his financial coffers and then return to Chicago. In the middle of my sophomore year, Fred took a job in a funeral home very close to where we lived, but for me it became a racist and sexist nightmare. Everything I had ingested that was good through Thomas Merton's writings was now usurped by Fred. Although I loved Fred and he loved me, his racism I could not deal with—I felt emotionally torn.

That school year brought many changes; Larry and I were no longer sexually and emotionally involved with each other, but succumbed to social pressure to date, which we did. I tolerated this painful situation as Larry and I drifted away from each other, and our relationship finally ended when he dropped out of high school to get married.

Dealing with my racism was soon thwarted because of Fred's influences—again my mother pawned me off on him. By this time, I had a large lab, and it became much larger when a local physician retired and his nurse gave me a lot of his medical equipment, including journals. By this time, Fred had brought me into the funeral business; he taught me how to embalm and my first embalming was with a dead dog that had been hit by a car and later helping Fred with human remains.

Knowing how to embalm, having a larger lab only added to my scientific interest, which included my childhood friend Tom who became interested in helping me with my experiments. Tom and I never had a sexual relationship; we had a more cerebral and scholarly relationship. During this time, I was researching the differences between molds and fungi. I wondered if bread mold would kill athlete's foot fungus. My father had athlete's feet, so I did a foot scraping and began growing athlete's foot fungus in a petri dish as well as bread mold in another petri dish. I thought I had cleaned the petri dishes satisfactorily to grow the organisms, but soon discovered I hadn't. As a result, what I grew in the fungus petri dish was an amalgam of undefined microorganisms. Although I didn't realize my mistake at the time, I entered the experiment in the local Science Fair at the insistence of my biology teacher.

Within a few months, Tom's hands become red, itchy and his skin began to peel, as an unknown fungus we had grown slowly infected both hands. He went to several physicians, and none was able to help. Finally, a neighbor told him about an old country doctor who had cured several friends of fungus. Tom saw the physician and after careful examination, the physician went into another room and made a salve. Within days, Tom's hands begin to heal and finally a few weeks later the fungus was gone. That was a relief for both of us, but the fungus did not deter our experiments in science.

Chapter 4

DESPAIR AND NOWHERE TO TURN

MY STUDIES OF THOMAS MERTON WERE NOT ONLY HELPING ME WORK through my racism but was also helping me develop prayer and contemplation practices. While trying to understand these practices, I came across an ad in a *Fate Magazine* about a group called the Rosicrucian's. I soon joined the Rosicrucian order, once I had money from being employed in a high school government work/study program. With the Rosicrucian's, I began studying various methods to alter my consciousness through visualization, contemplation, and meditation as well as alchemy. Merton's contemplative practices and the Rosicrucian's visualizations fit nicely with the pagan rituals my grandmother had taught me. However, these studies soon moved into the background because my brother Fred continued exposing me to his extreme racism and away from anything good and spiritual. This would drag on into my junior year of high school. I loved my brother, and I knew he loved me, but his racist and sexist hatred left me confused.

In the last half of my sophomore year, my father found a better paying job in a coal mine in the small western Kentucky town of Beaver Dam. My father and mother soon moved, leaving me with my grandmother as well as Fred and Delilah. However, at the end of my sophomore year my parents took me to live with them in Beaver Dam. I thought Fred was finally out of my life with his racist and sexist vitriol giving me the space I needed to pursue my contemplative and esoteric interest.

The only positive outcome of living in Beaver Dam was there was a Roman Catholic church nearby. Having a Catholic church so close allowed me to continue my studies in catechism, which eventually led to my baptism. Another asset living in this area was we lived about sixty miles from the Abbey of Gethsemani, where Thomas Merton was a monk. Visiting the Abbey often deepened my connection with the Trappist Order and especially trying to understand the spiritual presence deep within me.

The Trappist had a profound effect on me. I often considered joining the community after graduating from high school. However, uneasiness deep inside prevented me from making the move after I had a decisive dream. In the dream, I was walking on a path in front of the Abbey and came to a fork in the path. The right path led into the Abbey and the left path led away from the Abbey. I stopped at the fork and pondered my situation and took the left path leading away from the Abbey. However, over the years the thought of joining a religious community stayed with me.

The move to western Kentucky had the benefits of studying catechism as well as being near Thomas Merton. However, several months after the move, I was suddenly plunged into deep despair and depression when Fred and Delilah paid us a visit. They had moved to a small town on the Ohio River south of Louisville, Kentucky so Fred could complete his apprenticeship in the funeral business before moving back to Chicago. This move was a bad mistake because it did not afford the training he needed. The owner of the funeral home lied about how much yearly business came in and besides the preparation or embalming room was suited for the 1800s.

Fred fell into a deep depression, which also affected me. My moods dramatically shifted as I struggled with my sexual identity as well as trying to understand why Fred hated certain people so deeply. I had no idea at the time how close we were because his depression influenced me by triggering my deep inner struggles. It was as though our two minds were linked, and I was taking on his depression, which only magnified my own deep emotional uncertainties. I became morose, belligerent, self-absorbed, and started drinking and smoking marijuana as sexual thoughts and feelings I had suppressed began surfacing.

One day in a strange conversation that seemed to come out of nowhere, Fred began talking about the Nazi doctor Joseph Mengele, who was trying to create a master white race. I had never heard of this man before nor did I really understand what Nazis were. I knew my uncles fought the Germans in World

War II, and one of our uncle's helped to liberate Nazi concentration camps, but this was the first time I took notice of the word Nazi.

I had no idea who this Nazi doctor was or what Nazism really was until my senior year in high school. I began researching both the German Nazi party, the American Nazi party as well as the American Communist party and Communism in general. As I was researching the Nazis, a vague memory surfaced about a movie I had seen years earlier called *Mein Kampf.* The contents of the movie were so disturbing and sickening I totally put it out of my mind. The movie was about Hitler, the Nazis, and the mass extermination of people.

Unconsciously, I created a disconnect between the German people and the Nazis, but with what Fred was saying forced me to relive the contents of the movie all over again. This led me to find out who this Nazi doctor was, and I soon discovered his inhumane experiments. I began to understand that the Nazis and the KKK were on the same page; they hated people of color and supported slavery and mass murder. Although Communism was just as bad as Nazism when it came to mass murder, however, Communism did not have the racist component.

In researching Nazism, I soon became aware that their primary targets were Jewish people, political adversities, Gypsies, and gay people. I became confused as to who Jewish people were because my South Carolina relatives had talked about them negatively, but I knew who gay people were because I was gay. I wondered, why are Jews and gays hated so much to try to exterminate them all. I knew the KKK was bad, but Naziism was the apex of racism. I couldn't get it out of my mind the number of Jews the Nazis killed. It would be a few months before I met the first Jewish family I had ever encountered, and they would be pivotal in challenging my own racism.

Trying to get a handle on my inner struggles as well as my brother's insanity, I would retreat to my small lab in the basement where we lived in Beaver Dam, Kentucky in an attempt to occupy my thoughts with chemistry. My lab and science books were my only comfort as I kept my sexual identity hidden. My despair only intensified when I came home from school one day and found my science books missing. I asked my mother where they were, and she said, "Gary Wayne, I had your Daddy burn them because you are getting too many funny ideas in your head"—I was devastated. My only source of comfort and escape was gone as my interest in science, spirituality and religion took its toll.

I disassembled my lab, putting everything in boxes as disinterest in everything swallowed me and morbid darkness set in.

Turning to psychology to find out what was happening to me, I read as many psychology books as I could find in the school library. I continued to tumble deeper into despair and became so unruly, my parents sent me back to live with my maternal grandmother. At the time, psychology became a driving force in finding out how to deal with the uncertain sexuality ticking inside making my mood and outlook so dark.

This darkness lasted throughout my senior year; I gave up everything spiritual and scientific, except for psychology. With my lab equipment stored in boxes, I abandoned everything of who I was. I lost myself completely, turned to the theater and dove into dancing and acting. I pretended to be someone else trying to relieve the inner pain and struggles that was swallowing me.

Still trying to find answers to my conflicted life in psychology books, my life took a turn for the worse two months before graduation. My grandmother and I were visiting my friend Tom's grandmother who had been her friend for years. After several beers, the conversation turned to me. My grandmother said unlike my brothers, I was a problem child from the start, and it began with my birth. Without warning she told us, I was born dead. She said the physician on duty worked frantically trying to bring me to life. And after a long struggle, I came to life. With this new information, I was overwhelmed with more feelings of uncertainty about everything including who I was. I emotionally shut down, canceled my date for the senior prom and began drinking heavily.

Although I was struggling with my sexuality, my racism was beginning to take a turn. I was now free from Fred's negative influences and comments about how he hated certain people because he was back in Chicago. The first crack in my racism was when I became a clothing salesman for the 'Quality Shop' through the Christmas holiday. The Quality Shop was owned by the Steinbergs, and they were very nice to me, and I soon discovered they were Jewish. My experiences with the Steinbergs were very different from what my Union,

South Carolina relatives and Fred had told me about Jews. I had a cognitive disconnect because the Steinbergs were the first Jewish family I had ever known, and they were very nice people.

The Steinbergs were the first to put a crack in my racist attitudes because within a few weeks after graduating from high school I was dealing with another racial issue, African Americans. One night in the adjacent house on our property that was used for washing clothers and at one time housed my laboratory was the setting for a major change. I had changed the back room where my lab used to be to a dance and acting studio replete with an old piano.

I was playing the piano one evening when the door unexpectedly opened and there stood a black man whom at first, I didn't recognize. After a few moments, I recognized him; it was JC, a former high school basketball player that came to our school during integration. At the time, I had no black friends and felt extremely uncomfortable with him being in my presence. However, over the next few weeks, JC would drop by at night, and we would play the piano together. I was still uncomfortable with him but tolerated the situation.

One night, full of bourbon and a strong dose of racism from James Otis, I was drunk and ready for a confrontation. When I came home, I heard the piano playing, opened the door, and there sat JC at the piano with a big smile. A horrible confrontation ensued, and I ran JC off our property with a cacophony of racial slurs. Weeks later, I felt horrible guilt and shame over the incident, but never saw JC again. He just wanted to be my friend!

Although I never saw JC again, the impact of that encounter changed my life forever regarding racism. Within a few weeks, I was a freshman at Eastern Kentucky University and in this new environment, I began discarding everything racist I had been taught, plunging myself into the civil right movement. By my sophomore year, I had dealt with my racist attitudes and then found myself being challenged by the University's dorm director. I was called into his office and informed that there were so many male students that year because of the Vietnam War that new arrangements had to be made regarding housing. The friend whom I was going to room with drowned in Chicago that summer and the only roommate that was available needing to be placed was an African American. The dorm director asked me very gently if I would be willing to let a "colored boy" room with me. If not, they would try to find another arrangement such as rooming with two other students making it three to a room—not a good situation.

I thought for a few minutes and then decided since I'm now in the civil rights movements, this would be my first act in desegregation. I think my roommate's name was Jerry or something like that and we as well as others would be breaking down the black/white segregation barriers in the rooming situation. He was a fine roommate! However, that year with my involvement in the civil rights movement as well as interracially dating, my life would be threatened several times. These death threats brought me once again to the threshold of exploring and trying to understand death and the afterlife as it applied to my current situation.

Beginning in my senior year of high school and throughout this period, I began searching everything religious as it pertained to death and the afterlife. Not only working with Fred in the funeral business, which shaped my views of the afterlife, the Rosicrucians were also radically changing my views as well. With death, subtle insights continued surfacing that were very different from what Catholicism was teaching me. Somewhere in my inner world, I had an intense knowing there was no heaven or hell, but worlds without pain and suffering dotting many realities in which I wanted to explore and experience. I knew without question, there was a presence inside of me filled with indescribable love. Roman Catholicism at first gave me a religious identity and a foundation, but I was beginning to feel uneasy about some of the teachings and doctrines as well as its bloody history. Some teachings were okay; those about helping people, but some seemed too restrictive and judgmental, which was true with other Christian faiths as well.

By the end of my senior year in high school, I had totally rejected Catholicism's teachings on death and the afterlife but accepted many of its other teachings. I knew intuitively the world my step-grandfather went to after he died was not the Christian heaven or hell. I found myself arguing with clergy and other religious people about the afterlife. I told them there was no hell and the heaven they believed in did not exist. They called me an atheist, but I was far from being an atheist. I knew intuitively there were spiritual worlds all around us and knew without doubt that death was just a transition into those worlds. I knew these things but did not know how I knew them until I learned the hidden truth about my birth.

After learning I was born dead, death took on a new meaning. It was not the end of our earthly journey, but just another adventure. I soon realized, the glimpses I had of other worlds were not figments of my imagination, but real worlds I had lived in before I was born into this reality. For some reason, I felt I was asked or forced to come to this pain and suffering reality, which added to my feelings of alienation and not being from here. I also began to take note of how people perceived death and the afterlife. Some believed in a heaven and a hell. Some believed in reincarnation. Some believed there is nothing after death and some just didn't know. In all these beliefs, the single underlying emotion was fear; an intense fear of the pain of death or what may be experienced in the afterlife. This was one fear I did not have.

Dealing with the fact I was born dead sent me on a mission to find out why I came to this reality and how I could get back to the world I came from. I began reading many books from the Christian traditions on death and the afterlife when I was suddenly sidetracked by two books about the historical Jesus: *The Quest of the Historical Jesus* by Albert Schweitzer and *The Passover Plot* by Hugh Schonfield. These two books examined the historical facts regarding the Gospel's narrative of Jesus. This was the first time I had read anything that questioned certain stories in the life of Jesus as being false. I was stunned by this new information and had to find out more. My spiritual mission had now expanded to find out if other stories in the life of the historical Jesus were accurate.

I began a deeper study of the world's religious traditions, parapsychology, more esoteric philosophy, mysticism, magick and spirituality looking for more information on worlds and realms in the afterlife. I was trying to find out where I came from in the afterlife worlds. I was also searching for techniques and methods that would open portals into those parallel worlds. In this connection, I began an intense study of afterlife cases in parapsychology; I learned about séances and how to conduct them, but at the time, did not have the opportunity to put the techniques into practice. However, that would soon change. Not only was I trying to understand the afterlife, but I was also on a mission to find out more about the historical life of Jesus.

Chapter 5

A CHANGE IN PERSPECTIVE

MY FIRST YEAR OF COLLEGE SEVERAL FRIENDS AND I WERE HORSING around one weekend and decided to conduct a séance for fun because Halloween was just around the corner. We needed a medium to facilitate the séance and no one wanted to do it. Since I had some knowledge of séances from studying parapsychology, I decided to take the opportunity to be the intermediary because no one else stepped up to the plate. We then decided to contact President John F. Kennedy to find out where he was in the spirit world and how he was doing.

There were five of us—all males. We all sat around in a circle holding hands with a lit candle in the center. I closed my eyes, got very relaxed and summoned President Kennedy to come through me. Nothing happened so I continued to summon. After a long period, I began feeling strange and sensed something was coming into me. Suddenly, my awareness the conscious "I" began moving into the background; I became the observer. Something was in me, and it wasn't President Kennedy. It was a strange presence and when I tried to speak and tell my friends what was happening, I couldn't speak. When I finally spoke, it wasn't me speaking—it was the presence. It said, "Shem ma na lochi, Shem ma na lochi." It said this over and over. It took total control of my voice and my body. I began struggling to gain control of my body and finally came out of the experience, unsettled.

At the time, I thought I had been speaking in tongues but years later I found out that was not the case. In the oncoming years, I was still trying to find the translation of that phrase that came through me that night. Some thought it was Hebrew and some thought it was Aramaic, but it still didn't fit with those languages. However, I finally found the answer decades later, after writing an article for *New Dawn* magazine, "Inhabitants of the Imaginal Realm" (Duncan, Vol. 10). In the article, I recounted the story of my experience. Shelia Hoffmann, an Australian clairvoyant, contacted one of the editors of the magazine and told him what the translation of the message was. She had spent quite a bit of time in Taiwan and learned Mandarin. She said the words "Shem ma na lochi" is Mandarin, and its translation is "What are you trying to do?" This translation made sense because we were trying to perform a séance and didn't really understand what we were doing.

Although at first, I thought I was speaking in tongues, but something didn't feel right. As I mulled over the experience it was becoming clear that some kind of spirit had taken over my body. And since I struggled to reclaim control of my body, I began to entertain the spirit was nefarious, an evil spirit or a demon. Because of this experience, my interest in psychic phenomena, mediumship, spirit possession and the afterlife accelerated. I knew I was on to something and seriously began studying more religious views about spirits, the transition of the soul into the afterlife, especially the Egyptian Book of the Dead and later the Tibetan Book of the Dead. This study eventually broadened to include karma and reincarnation. The séance experience and my studies of the afterlife were preparing me for some unusual experiences with my maternal grandmother that would profoundly impact my understanding of the dying and death process.

Spring semester of that year, the veil between the material world and the spiritual world was dramatically raised. I had a strange conversation with my maternal grandmother. As we spoke by phone, I got a strange feeling she knew something was about to happen. Unlike other conversations I had had with her, she ended by telling me goodbye as if it was final.

Two weeks later, I awoke with a feeling of dread. Later that day when I returned to the dorm, I saw a message on the bulletin board to call home, which was not unusual. I knew instantly my grandmother had died, and she had. I was puzzled! How did I know she had died? Did that sense of knowing have something to do with my own situation of being born dead or my spirit possession during the séance?

Later at her funeral, I discovered she had called all her grandchildren and told them goodbye. She knew intuitively weeks before she died that she was going to die. Not only was I mystified about how my grandmother knew about her impending death, but how did I know she was dead before I had confirmed it. I knew this insight had something to do with my own entrance into this world, which laid the foundation for being opened to communicate with spirits. These events propelled me to find out as much as I could about psychic connections, my own death at birth, spirits in general and the intuitive signs that signals of one's impending death. Trying to figure out these experiences only drove me into a deeper level of inquiry, "How is the reality we experience put together and why is there pain and suffering"?

As I was absorbed in the study of the afterlife, the impact of the séance, my grandmother's death, how reality is structured and my sexuality—I remained in a state of confusion. Since my junior year in high school, my sexuality was heading for a major shift. I was away from James Otis but his influence regarding my sexuality had been shaped by him giving me money for sexual favors. He encouraged me to experience as much sex as I could with different men. He also informed me I could make money by selling my body to older men.

At first, I had a problem with this but by the time I was a senior in high school my thoughts had changed. James Otis had schooled me on the cue's men would give if they wanted to have a sexual encounter. And since James Otis was already paying me, I thought I could make more money from other older men. This became evident when my parents sent me back to live with my grandmother to complete my senior year of high school. I took a Trailways bus to Louisville and then a Greyhound to where my grandmother lived. I was using the restroom at the Greyhound bus station when I noticed several men watching me while I was standing at the urinal. As I walked out of the restroom several men eyed me and one older man followed me.

I sat down on one of the bench-type seats and within seconds the man that followed me set nearby. He glanced over toward me and took some money out of his wallet and put it in his shirt pocket. He got up and walked out of the bus station and shortly I followed him. I saw him standing near one of the doors and I went in the opposite direction and stopped to look at an advertisement. Within seconds he was beside me making small talk and then told me how gorgeous I was, and he knew I had a "beautiful cock". He said he would like to show me off to some friends. He then put the money into my shirt pocket and the next thing I knew I was in his car. He drove me to an apartment building; we went down a flight of steps into a small apartment. In the living room were several men having sex with several teenage boys. And the next thing I knew I was being fondled and told how beautiful I was.

After the encounter, he drove me back to the Greyhound bus station, playing with me all the way. I got out of his car with the money and off to live with my grandmother. This experience gave me the knowledge of how to peddle my wares to make money. James Otis had taught me how to be a prostitute by giving me small amounts of money. Now with twenty dollars in my pocket, I knew I could make more with my body. That prostituting experience was at the beginning of my senior year of high school and would last a little over three years. In that period, not only was I a prostitute but later found myself in the pornography business as well.

Also, in my senior year, my focus changed; I got more into dance especially classical ballet and drama. During this time, I met a director of a local ballet theater. He was an older man who used my body, paid well, and made promises to help get me into the dance business. Every time I was in Louisville, he would put me up in the Brown Hotel, and I thought I had a friend in him, but his promises never amounted to anything.

Throughout my freshman and sophomore years at Eastern Kentucky University, my life was being shaped by the Vietnam War, the civil rights movement, and my sexuality. It seemed that every sexual predator was after me and eventually found myself in many gay orgies and being either filmed or photographed in explicit sexual acts. The pornography I was in always ended up in New York City for sale, that is what I was told. Not only was I dealing with these issues, my parents and I were in constant struggles. At times, my father would not speak to me; we were always at logger heads. The main issue was I did not want to go into the funeral business.

My college major at the time was psychology with two minor areas: drama and dance. After several months in drama and working on sets, I decided to drop drama and focus on psychology as my primary major with two minor areas: dance and philosophy. Philosophy added a new dimension, especially existentialism. I was exposed to the writings of Jean Paul Sartre and his play *No Exit*, which had a deep impact on me. It presented another view of the afterlife especially what hell was like! Hell from this perspective is a reality in which three people were caught in a room, all having desires and wants that cannot be satisfied and were stuck in this situation forever. This view of hell made sense to me; it was vastly different from the Christian beliefs but fit with the fearful pain and suffering reality I experienced every day.

With psychology, I found myself studying both psychoanalysis and behaviorism two areas that were antagonistic with each other. I had already been counseling with some of my gay friends around sexual issues. Like many gay men at the time, I was able to hide behind pretending to be straight by dating women. At the time, I had been dating several white and black women keeping my true sexual orientation hidden.

One night with an African American woman I had been dating, I was in the heat of passion and was ready to have sex, which would have been the first woman I would have had sex with. When I was ready to have sex, she looked into my eyes and said, "I want to have your baby!" I lost my erection and pulled away from her. I then realized women just want to breed and I wasn't going to have anything to do with it. I would never bring a soul into this violent and painful reality. Besides, I had already been blamed by a woman, whom I used to dance with accusing me of getting her pregnant. She even gave her baby girl my last name and sent a photo of the little girl to my mother. I had never had sex with her or any woman. I was now seeing the full picture about women and quickly moved away from them as best I could. However, that was a bit of a problem because I was part of the civil rights movement, and several women were my dance partners.

One African American woman whom I was involved with at the time became the focus of racist slurs and threats. One day a white male student, whom

I thought was my friend, said to me, "I saw you with that 'nigger' again. One day when you and that 'nigger bitch' walks out of the student union, I'll be waiting for you hiding in the ravine. I'll put you two in the crosshairs and put a bullet between both of your eyes." I could not believe what I was hearing and after that day was very cautious when we were in public.

Alongside my relationship with African American women, I had another relationship with an African American man. Although I had had sex with two black men while I was being filmed for pornography, as well as with Pepper, a black playmate when I was in the sixth grade, however, this new relationship was different. He and I were blazing new trails in both the gay and non-gay civil rights movements forming a serious black/white relationship, which was my first adult gay relationship. At the time, black/white sexual relationships were relatively new and few in the gay community. Many of my white gay so-called friends would taunt me for being with a black man. At the time, these types of relationships were looked down on. All these relationships ended with summer break for it would be another year before I attended college again.

That summer would bring more conflict between me and my father for insisting I go into the funeral business with my brother. The conflict got so out of hand; my father told me to get out of his house. This was the first time he kicked me out of the house and told me if I didn't go into the funeral business, he would stop helping me with college tuition. I loaded up my suitcase and hitch-hiked to Louisville knowing my director friend would help me.

I had nowhere to stay, and my director friend of a local ballet theater said he would help me. Again, he put me up in the Brown Hotel for three days telling me he was working on finding me a place to live so he could get me into the world of dance. On the third day, he came to the hotel room, had sex with me and then walked out the door telling me to get out of the hotel room—I was on my own. My father had kicked me out and now the director had kicked me out; I was on the streets with nowhere to go.

Lugging my suitcase and umbrella down the street wondering what I would do, I soon walked into an old friend Twiggy. I had had sex with his bisexual brother many times. Twiggy said I could live with him and Tina, but little did I know Tina ran a house of prostitution. She was lesbian herself and had several male prostitutes living with her and sex was always happening. Most of the men I had sex with paid well but a few didn't. All the prostitutes had been kicked out of their homes because they were gay except for me.

Not only was I prostituting but found myself in stolen cars and in places I could be killed just by having the wrong expression on my face. I was getting to the point of dreading selling my body, which was heightened when one of the prostitutes I became friends with committed suicide. On the hills of his death, I found myself in a situation where I was almost killed.

One of the male prostitutes had rolled one of his paying client's and the next night he came for revenge. I was sitting in the living room when shots rang out. Bullets were hitting the side of the house. I jumped to the floor and crawled beside of my bed underneath the window to keep from being shot. As I laid there in fear, I knew I was going to die and begin thinking what dying was going to feel like. After what seemed to be an eternity the gun shots finally stopped. The next day with little money, I found a room in a rooming house and moved in. The place was a mess with dog shit all around but knew I needed to be there for a while to be safe. My only work was prostitution, but I decided since I had some psychology under my belt, I might be able to find a job in one of the hospitals.

There were two hospitals close by, so I put my application in both and was hired by Kentucky Baptist Hospital as a Psychiatric Attendant, assisting with electro-convulsive treatments or shock treatment like my mother had had. Still with little money before I got paid, I hit the streets again. It was July 20, 1969 when I had my last prostitute encounter for money, I just couldn't take it anymore. The man paid me, I got out of his car and walked into the rooming house. As I was heading up the stairs to my dirty room, I passed a room on the first floor with the door open, and the TV was on. As I walked past the room, I heard someone saying on TV, "That's one small step for a man, one giant leap for mankind." Not only did we make it to the moon, but that night ended my over three-year stent not only with prostitution but pornography as well. Also, after getting my first paycheck from the hospital, I moved to another rooming house that was clean and had access to a phone.

What I found interesting, throughout those years of prostitution most of the men who bought me were married men. In one incident, I was walking in front of the Brown Theater in Louisville, when I saw a man with a woman coming toward me whom I recognized. Several weeks earlier he had bought me for a few hours of sex play, but when he spotted me, he turned his head away pretending not to recognize me. I knew the woman was his wife because on the night we tricked, he took out his wallet and showed me his family, which included his children and wife. Showing me family photos was not unusual for a lot of married men I had sex with.

In ending my over three-year stent in prostitution and pornography, I also had to deal with James Otis, the sexual predator who abused me and got me into this business. My first opportunity came in October 1969 when someone gave him my address in Louisville, Kentucky. James Otis sent me a letter, wanted to meet me, and I agreed to meet him in a downtown restaurant. Before we even ordered our meal, I told him to get out of my life and never contact me again. He was totally shocked when I got up from the table and left. I thought he was out of my life for good but the anger toward him would not abate. I ruminated on all the unkind things I would like to do to him. Day after day my disgust toward him raged deep inside.

Five years later, I decided to confront him once again but discovered this was not an easy thing to do because I needed a sound strategy to eliminate him completely from my life. From the letter he sent when I lived in Louisville, I knew he was living in Cincinnati, Ohio. At the time, I had been living in Cincinnati for a few years with my lover Steph and finally tracked him down and went for a visit. At first, I was very uncomfortable being in his presence, and wanted to attack him on the spot but decided not to because the timing wasn't right. So, I decided to play cat at the mouse hole and patiently waited until my strategy was completely formalized. I pretended to be his friend but loathed every second being in his presence. By being patient, it took another seven years to create the strategy for my final confrontation. The only way I could be around him was to be in a drunken state; I simply loathed him. So, throughout this period pretending to be his friend, I stayed in a state of intoxication waiting until I was ready to blast him.

During that period, I would see him off and on in a gay bar; he was now a severe sickening alcoholic. I discovered he was worse than when I first met him; he hated everything and was now a bigger sexual predator, racist, a bigot and totally amoral. At first, I would drink heavily trying to block him out completely but then began slowly taking my time to drink my glass of wine as I contemplated my strategy for the final attack. He had no idea I was keeping myself sober, so when the opportunity came to attack him, I was clear minded.

Being a racist, James Otis would blast me over and over for interracially dating that began when I was in the civil rights movement. I knew I now had the segue that would lead to the final confrontation but had to wait for the exact moment and it finally came. On the final day of reckoning, he began making racist comments as usual but this time he focused on Daryl the African American man I was dating who eventually became my spouse. It was that day everything came together just like the cat getting the mouse. I felt the rage rising inside me, and when he called Daryl a "Nigger", I lost it.

In the gay bar with everyone listening I laid into him, telling him what a despicable, sickening creature he was, a pathetic alcoholic, low life racist, bigot and sexual pervert for sexually molesting me and other innocent children. I laid bare everything he had done to me calling him an amoral, sickening creature who should be in prison. Others in the bar just watched me blasting him. One bar patron into S&M and bondage told me I should not talk to him that way, in which case I blasted him and left the bar never to return. In early 1982, James Otis was out of my life for good. I felt complete and emotionally lighter; a whole load of shit was now off my shoulders and out of my life for good!

Chapter 6
ANOTHER MOUNTAIN TO CLIMB

AFTER COMPLETING TWO YEARS OF COLLEGE AS A PSYCHOLOGY MAJOR, my family continued pressuring me to become a funeral director, creating a family business. At the time, the requirements to become a mortician (this term is slowly becoming obsolete) included two years of college, two years of mortuary school and two years apprenticeship. The apprenticeship could be completed before or after mortuary school. If completed, I would have two licenses, one as a funeral director and one as an embalmer. Working with Fred over the years, I learned the ins and outs of the funeral business, and only needed a few more months to complete my apprenticeship.

After about four months of being kicked out of my parents' home and not communicating with them, I decide to call to find out how things stood. My mother was glad to hear from me, but my father was still distant, however, he did invite me to Thanksgiving dinner which I took him up on. My father's soft spot was breads, so I went to a bakery and bought him several loafs of a variety of breads to soften things between us. I found it interesting on the Thanksgiving trip nothing was said about me becoming part of the funeral business.

Because of our conflicts and being kicked out of my parents' home, I took that year off from college. This gave me time to sort through a lot of issues, however, before I could come up with any solutions, I was drafted. The induction process was demeaning and sickening. On the medical form, I disclosed I had homosexual tendencies and the Army psychiatrist, which was very effeminate, told me he didn't believe me. He asked me to name a gay bar in Louisville in which case I named several as well as some in Cincinnati. He still said he didn't believe me and asked if I had been in the hospital for any medical condition. I told him I had been hospitalized for a stomach ulcer in the past. He then told me to get a letter from my physician, which I did and was deferred from serving in the military. I think on some level, he really knew I was gay, but didn't want to defer me because of my sexual orientation, nevertheless, he needed some other excuse to keep a gay man out of the military.

Up to that point, I had about two years in the Army ROTC at Eastern Kentucky University, which I hated. Even though the Army psychiatrist said he didn't believe me, it was most likely because I am masculine and didn't appear gay but to be on the safe side, he found a way to keep a possible gay man out of the Army. Intuitively, I felt sexual vibes from the psychiatrist and my "gaydar" knew he was also gay, and I felt his actions were in some way to hide his own sexual orientation.

I was so disgusted with the induction process and having anything to do with the military; I burned my draft card. Because of the ordeal, within weeks, I became very sick battling once again stomach issues that hadn't flared up in years. By early February, I was feeling better, and my father called to tell me Fred and Delilah were coming for a visit in March. He emphasized since I was sick, I should come home right away so they could help me heal. He also said he could help me get a job locally. So, I packed up and headed back to my parents because my father finally invited me back home. However, when I got there, Fred and Delilah were already there. They along with my father set me up to go to Chicago to finish my apprenticeship in the funeral business. They had deceived me!

☆☆☆

I begin working with Fred in his funeral home, a funeral livery service and another funeral home on alternate weekends as well as working in a nearby hospital with terminal cancer patients. I was immersed in the professions of dying, death, and bereavement. With bereavement, my psychology background came in handy with grieving families. Although, working with bereavement was very satisfying, the afterlife was beginning to interest me more after having several unusual experiences in the funeral home.

One day, Fred and I were embalming a body when all of a sudden, I quickly turned away from the embalming table and looked around the preparation room. I had an uneasy feeling we were being watched. At the time, I didn't say anything to Fred. Later, the same thing happened again. This time I mentioned it to Fred. He said many times while preparing a body; he felt the soul of that person was watching the procedures. After that, I became cognizant of those feelings, and they happened many times. I became very aware when these souls were watching and decided to call them "the watchers".

As I was adjusting to the watchers, another unusual experience happened. Fred and Delilah went out of town for the weekend and left me in charge of the funeral home. It so happened, we had a viewing. After the family of the deceased had left the funeral home, I proceeded to lock up and turn off the lights. I was checking the back door near the preparation room and a basement storage room that contained unclaimed cremation urns dating back to the 1930s, when I started having strange sensations. I began feeling there was something behind me as I walked down the long hallway to the office. As I picked up walking speed, I started feeling a warm sensation on the nap of my neck that rapidly shifted to an ice-cold breath. I did not look behind me, but careened through the office, ran up the stairs to the apartment where we lived, and shut the door behind me. The cold breath sensation was gone. Years later, I told Fred about the experience, and he said he had the same experience as well.

Some of the remains we prepared for burial were victims of suspicious deaths (murder). I often wondered what those souls thought watching us prepare their bodies for viewing because at times, I could feel their presence. I also wondered how they perceived the people who killed them and wondered if the murderer could feel the presence of their victims as I was feeling. Thinking about victims and murderers, I began questioning, what are the psychological differences between mass murderers, serial killers and murders resulting from rage. I also wondered if the murdered victims haunted the places where they were murdered or haunted the people who murdered them. I kept these questions to myself but entertained them every time we prepared a body of a suspicious death.

My father told me early on that if I didn't go into the funeral business, he would only help me financially with the first two years of college because that's what was required to go to mortuary school. So, knowing this, I secretly prepared myself by taking a two-year specialized training program in analytical chemistry through the technical school ICS. I already had a lab, so the only thing I needed was course instructions. Studying part-time, in between all my other studies with an extension took me a little over three years to complete the training. In case I decided to pursue psychology rather than the funeral business, I would have the necessary training to get a job in the chemical industry that would help pay my way through college.

I finally completed my apprenticeship in the funeral business, but decided rather than enrolling in mortuary school, I would go back to college to continue my studies in psychology. I had saved enough money to pay my tuition and then some. As my father had warned earlier, he did eventually cut me off financially. I went back to Eastern Kentucky University for the last time. Although my father was cutting me off financially, he did give me some money for food. My decision not to go into the funeral business caused a major family disruption replete with arguments and the silent treatment—I was on the outs.

Not only had I decided to continue my education in psychology, but also, I was dealing with a major internal crisis—my sexual orientation. As I was coming to grips with my sexuality after not being believed by the Army psychiatrist, I decided to seek counsel, so I went to my parish priest Father McGuire in the hope of receiving guidance. When I explained my situation and asked what I should do, Father McGuire said, "Walk out the door and never come back." That day, I was kicked out of the Roman Catholic Church for simply being who I was.

In distress and confusion, I turned to my parents, hoping to get some comfort. However, the decision not to continue in the funeral business had created a huge family rift, and now with my sexual orientation, my fate was sealed. When I told my mother by phone I was homosexual, she started crying. My father in the background asked what was going on and she told him I was homosexual; then I heard my father say, "He's not welcome in my house again. I don't have a son!" My parents kicked me out of their lives as well as the family—I no longer had a family and no longer had a church. My family and I did not speak to each other for five years and then slowly began mending our relationship. However, I never returned to the dysfunctional and corrupt Roman Catholic Church; I was through with that pathetic controlling institution.

Because of these decisions, my financial situation was dire; I could no longer continue college, nor did I have a place to live. I still had a month to live in the dorm but after that I would be on the streets. In the mix of confusion, I realized I had one option, Steph. I had met Steph in a gay bar in Cincinnati and he had been hounding me to become his lover. He wanted to find an apartment and move in together. Steph was the last person I would consider being my partner because he was too effeminate, and later after we began living together, I discovered he was a bigoted racist. To get under my skin, he would make racist comments about African American babies—I absolutely had no love for him. However, the bind I found myself in—living with him was the best option.

At the beginning, we lived with several of his siblings until we found a place of our own. I soon discovered Steph was dishonest and was cheating on me, but because I had nowhere to go, I tolerated the situation and began cheating as well. I felt if I didn't do what he asked, I would not have a place to live. Within a year, I found a job at Doctor Scholl's Shoes in Cincinnati. Now with money in my pocket, I began moving away from him emotionally and within four years I stopped having sex with him altogether. Unlike Steph, I was exclusively involved in a five-year clandestine affair with a married man as well as a non-sexual emotional intellectual relationship with a Jewish woman. The relationship between Steph and I was totally deceitful and dishonest and was glad it eventually ended.

I had completed my training in analytic chemistry from ICS and was now looking for a position with a chemical company. I worked for Doctor Scholl's for one year and during that time, started taking classes at the University of Cincinnati (UC); at the time they had an excellent psychology department. I knew I would eventually find a position in the chemical industry, but until that happened, I drifted from mindless job to mindless job, and finally became an electrical repairman for a company repairing spot welders. I made enough money to continue paying for my classes at U.C. in the pursuit of a bachelor's degree in psychology.

After two years of financial struggle, I finally landed a position with USI Chemical Company in the summer of 1973. The employment package included college reimbursement for any area of academic concentration—I was set. I worked in analytical chemistry for a short period and then was promoted to polymer research, which was much more exciting and more money. USI allowed me the freedom to make major research decisions, which lead to two patents. With their college reimbursement program, I completed my bachelor's degree in psychology and a master's degree in corrections with an emphasis on counseling as well as research. The reason I chose corrections was while working in the funeral business, I became interested in the psychology of murderers. My interest was how to control this type of criminal behavior. I began looking into animal studies on controlling behavior by inserting electrodes into specific areas of the brain, which did work on some animal behaviors. Although at the time, this procedure was not used on intractable criminals because of several issues—moral, ethical, and we didn't completely understand how the brain worked as well as human rights issues, we just couldn't experiment on criminals.

Part 11

Dramatic Shift:
Spiritual Road Ahead

Chapter 7

BACK TO THE SPIRITUAL

WHILE PURSING MY ACADEMIC DEGREES AND WORKING IN THE CHEMICAL industry, I was also involved in psychological and neuro-physiological animal research as well. To offset the heavy load in academia and research, I began refocusing once again on spirituality. I was now glad the dysfunctional Roman Catholic Church had kicked me out for being gay. Being ousted for who I am told me exactly what this religious institution was truly about, an organization of deceit, bigotry and cruelty that had murdered millions of people throughout its history all in the name of Jesus. However, without a religion, I felt free to explore a variety of new spiritual traditions.

It was during this period I began to reassess my maternal grandmother's nature religion and began to move into witchcraft also known as Wicca. I soon found a coven, was trained, and initiated into the Scottish Wiccan tradition. I practiced this religion for about two years finding it not as exciting and rewarding as I once thought. Also, I discovered Wicca was not the witchcraft my grandmother practiced because modern Wicca was created mainly by Gerald Gardner in the late 1930s—not an ancient religion at all.

While practicing Wicca, I became acquainted with an interesting podiatrist at Doctor Scholl's Shoes where I worked, whom was into everything metaphysical, magickal and the occult in general. Our conversations were deep, and I was able to confide in him about the spiritual experiences I had had throughout my life. I disclosed my maternal grandmother was a pagan Celtic Christian, told stories about and practiced witchcraft, magick and the shamanic traditions. I also disclosed I had studied with the Rosicrucian's which eventually turned me to the Kabbalah. I began studying the Kabbalah in 1969 after leaving prostitution and pornography. The podiatrist told me where I could find books on various occult topics: a bookstore called Dawn of Light. Dawn of Light had a wealth of information on the topics I was interested in as well as other esoteric and mystical traditions.

Browsing the various sections in the store opened new horizons in Hinduism, Taoism, Buddhism, and ceremonial magick. I had a smorgasbord of spiritualties to sample and explore. I was also looking for books on the historical Jesus but found none in the area I was looking for. I read more about the Wiccan religion, shamanism, Native American religions, magick and more on the Kabbalah. In studying these topics, I soon discovered I didn't enjoy being a part of a group or coven because my personality was more in tuned with being a solitary practitioner. There were too many egos to deal with in pagan and other magickal and esoteric groups.

In the Dawn of Light bookstore, I also found many books on parapsychology, an old interest from studying with the Rosicrucian's, the séance experience I had in college as well as various forms of meditation. I began studying and practicing what Janice Dean Willis (1972) called Tibetan Buddhist Diamond Light meditations. These meditations were very different from Kabbalistic meditations I had studied and practiced since 1969. With these meditations under my belt, I decided to explore other meditations and soon found Transcendental Meditation. These meditation practices were somewhat different from Kabbalistic pathworking meditations in which imagery was used. However, I soon discovered that Buddhist Tibetan Tantra meditations also used imagery but with a different slant than the Kabbala. These meditations laid the foundation to begin investigating various out-of-body experience methods, which eventually led to studying and experimenting with Bob Monroe's original roll out technique and later the Hemi-Sync system.

Although I had moved away from the funeral business and working with the terminally ill, I found new books at Dawn of Light that rekindled my interest in dying, death and the afterlife. With this renewed interest, I studied thanatology (the study of dying and death) in several of my undergraduate classes with an emphasis on Kubler-Ross coupled with Ernest Becker's *The Denial of Death*. In graduate school, I studied sociologist Anselm Strauss' work on terminal illness, grief and dying. I also studied Karlis Osis' work on deathbed phenomenon as well as Raymond Moody's work on near-death-experiences.

I finally completed my degree in psychology with a strong interest in sexual disorders, character disorders and murders. I discovered certain character disorders coupled with psychosis were contributing factors in the personality structure of murderers, such as mass murderers and serial killers. I also discovered that a personality type called authoritarian personality was linked to violent sexual crimes as well as violent criminal behavior in general. Some of the research I studied indicated this personality type was responsible for the mass killings in Nazi Germany.

To pursue this interest, I began working on a master's degree in Corrections with an emphasis on counseling and research into violent criminal behavior, and the possible control of this behavior through brain implants. At the time, brain implants were only being investigated through animal research. However, after a year into the master's program researching authoritarian personality as it related to mass murderers and serial killers, I found myself in an emotional impasse. I had read many clinical case studies and histories on these types of murderers and had interviewed murderers and violent criminals. I could not stomach the gruesome nature of these cases and began having second thoughts about working with this population. I knew I had to get out of this field when I found myself checking and rechecking the window locks and door locks to my second-floor apartment. Something had shifted in my soul; I was becoming more sensitive to the pain and suffering of others.

I needed a way out of this dilemma, but knew I had to complete my coursework and thesis leading to my master's degree. My dilemma was solved while interning at a halfway house. Several inmates wanted to complete their high school education by taking the GED exam. Their obstacle was math and the only staff member who had worked with math extensively was me, so I began tutoring math.

Tutoring math brought back my interest in the physical sciences, especially a hobby I had had since childhood—amateur astronomy. Finding myself once again in a career impasse, I had a long talk with a chemical engineer, fellow amateur astronomer and telescope maker. We decided since working with criminals was out of the question, the best route was to combine my interest in chemistry, astronomy, statistics, and psychology and figure out what to do with that combination.

The problem was soon solved, when I read a book by Gerald K. O'Neil on space colonization. Almost immediately, I began putting together plans on how to engineer space habitats for work environments. After several years in the chemical industry receiving two patents in polymer chemistry and two college degrees, I began pursuing a Ph.D. in Social Psychology. Within the first week of my doctoral studies, I found a professor interested in space colonization and he became my academic advisor.

My research and teaching scholarships could not pay for all my school debts, so I took a position as a lab researcher in teratology funded by grants at the Institute for Developmental Research a division of Children's Hospital of Cincinnati. Teratology is the study of congenital abnormalities and abnormal formations, and the area I worked in was behavioral teratology. My life was now about to take another drastic change.

The Institute for Developmental Research brought me back into the area of animal research, I had been out of for two years because of severe asthma and allergies. Rather than directly experimenting with animals, I was now checking data charts hung on mice cages for a caffeine study as well as another study focusing on red food dyes. I was also counting specific brain cells in mice after dissection looking for cell abnormalities resulting from a specific red food dye.

Every morning before sitting down at the microscope, I would go to the lower level of the Institute to check the recorded weights of experimental mice for the caffeine study. On my way back to the lab, I would stroll around the compound looking at all the experimental animals. I connected with a goat that had the most beautiful coat I had ever seen. The fur was a mixture of shades of white, tans and browns. For some reason I blocked out the fact the goat was an experimental animal.

One morning, after checking data charts, I strolled around the compound to talk to my goat friend. When I got to the goat's stall, I became confused when noticing two men, one in the stall and the other at the stall's open door. The goat had been euthanized and was slated for dissection. Apprehending what was taking place, something shifted in my awareness; an insight flooded in, I had never entertained before. At that moment, I realized over the years, I had been a part of a research industry that was cruel and caused needless pain and suffering to these defenseless animals.

This awareness changed the way I perceived these creatures; that day I decided to leave animal research and never experiment on animals again. My awareness regarding animal research changed forever. Animals are sentient beings we share this planet with, and they need to be respected as fellow creatures. That goat had changed my life forever, moving me into a new state of awareness. Within months after moving away from animal research, the asthma and allergies caused by animals totally lifted and never returned.

Shifting away from animal research, I began looking for other means to augment my meager university salary. With a few months left on my two-year contract at the Institute, I found a part-time teaching position in a technical college. I was also approached by Father Wayland Milton an Episcopal Priest to become part a community outreach program as a counselor at his church. Since I was using the church's facilities, I would charge a small fee for my services. Under Father Milton's supervision, this arrangement worked out well because it allowed me to refine my counseling skills, which I had used with criminals at the halfway house.

My counseling skills came in handy shortly before leaving the Institute for Developmental Research. A co-worker in another department discovered I knew something about parapsychology and engaged me in a conversation about unusual occurrences taking place in her home. Every day when the family left the house for work and school, strange activities would occur throughout the house during their absence. When they returned home, every room in the house would be in disarray. Cabinet doors would be opened, and the contents would be on the floor. Closet doors would be opened, and clothes would be thrown about the rooms. Dresser drawers would be pulled out with contents scattered about the room.

I told the co-worker what appeared to be happening was the family was experiencing a poltergeist phenomenon. With that information, she asked if I would investigate. I soon discovered a highly dysfunctional family with major conflicts between the mother (my co-worker) and her pubescent daughter. From my research in parapsychology, I knew the problem was the conflicts between mother and daughter as well as the daughter's internal conflicts revolving around puberty. The daughter in this instance was experiencing major sexual tensions over her emerging sexuality creating major identity crises, which resulted in the externalizations of her psychic energies producing the poltergeist activities.

I gave the mother my assessment and asked if there was another household where her daughter could live for a while. Her ex-husband, the daughter's father, was out of the question; he did not want to be burdened with his daughter because his new wife did not like her. So, it was decided the daughter should go to Arizona and live with the mother's sister during summer break. While the daughter was in Arizona, the poltergeist activities came to an abrupt halt. This was my first parapsychological counseling and investigation case, and it was a success.

☆☆☆

During this period, my advising professor who was interested in space colonies was at a conference and met several people from the Johnson Space Center in Houston, Texas. He told them about me, and I was soon scheduled for an interview to work on a project called the Space Operations Center. I would do basic research on creating work habitats that would facilitate social interactions with work crews in space stations, which would lead to my doctoral dissertation. In October 1979, I was interviewed successfully at Johnson Space Center. The decision was made I would start work as an intern beginning January 1981.

In conjunction with my interest in space science, I also found counseling very interesting. So, while counseling at the Episcopal Church, I began working with sexual issues and decided I needed training that was more specialized. So before leaving for Houston, I took sex therapy training with the Department of Psychiatry at the University of Kentucky College of Medicine. I had no idea how valuable the training would eventually become.

Throughout this period, Steph, who was my life partner at the time, and I were heading for a breakup; I simply could not stand him anymore. Although we were breaking up, we would still be connected with each other for another year. A friend of ours who lived in Houston begged us to relocate there. So, by the end of December 1980, I was in Houston waiting to be called to begin my internship in early 1981. As it turned out, the political climate had drastically changed, project funds were not appropriated, and the internship fell through. I was stuck in Houston for three months, could not find work because I was either over-qualified or under-qualified. I finally found a job performing statistical analysis for a commercial real estate company. However, within two weeks, I was out of work because the company fell into bankruptcy.

Disheartened and not knowing where to turn or what to do, I drove to a beach near Galveston. My life had fallen apart, it was in shambles; I began entertaining suicide by driving my car into the gulf. Sitting in my car starring at the moon's reflection on the gulf water, watching the waves roll in changing the dark water into foamy off-white and then receding back into the dark gulf stream.

I sat for a long time just starring aimlessly, asking why my life was in such shambles, and why I could not find stable work when Houston was in an employment boom. Staring into the moon's reflection on the water, my eyes slowly drifted up to the beautiful round bright moon suspended in the night sky. Then stillness flooded my car, as calmness overcame me. The inner presence that came to me in the mountains when I was seven years old returned after years of absence, accompanied with a voice penetrating deep into the center of my mind. In a whisper the voice said, "Everything will be alright, go back to Cincinnati and start over." Bursting into tears, I sat in silence. The next day, I journeyed back to Cincinnati not knowing what my future would hold. I resumed the teaching position in the technical college and continued my counseling practice at the Episcopal Church. Although working, I was still depressed; my life felt meaningless, the suicidal thoughts were gone, and I was on a slow rebound.

Chapter 8
Building a Workable Toolkit

Several months before leaving for Houston, I met my future life-partner and later my spouse, Daryl Coston. Our relationship became very close during my stay in Houston. He was the only one I talked with regarding my situation with NASA. He was there when I needed him and my return to Cincinnati brought us closer. We eventually committed to each other in March 1983; during that period, I was restructuring my counseling practice. At the time, unbeknownst to us, the move to a committed relationship added safety to our lives because AIDS was just beginning to spread.

My counseling practice at the Episcopal Church was at first limited to sex counseling and therapy with the gay and Appalachian communities. Moreover, counseling within the church's outreach program gave me the opportunity to work with spiritual issues as well. Working with these issues allowed me to refine my counseling skills and broaden my clinical practice. I soon realized, I needed more training in counseling and psychotherapy, so I enrolled in college once again. I also needed more office space, so early 1983, I left the Episcopal Church and set up a private practice. By this time, Father Melton was no longer at the church because he took an assignment in another parish, leaving me to phase out the community outreach program.

While setting up my private practice, Ohio passed a counseling licensure law, and as a result I became licensed. After licensure and further training, my psychotherapy practice expanded. I specialized in areas of traditional and trans-personal psychotherapy, sex therapy and counseling, parapsychological counseling as well as working with various psychotic populations. I was also beginning a lengthy training program in both Freudian and Jungian analysis and psychotherapy. This analytical training allowed me to refine and shift my early skills as a stage hypnotist into using those hypnotic skills in therapeutic age regression. My sex counseling and therapy practice also expanded, to include sex education, sexual abuse of children and adult survivors, paraphilias, which are unusual sexual deviations, desires, attractions, and practices as well as working with sexually transmitted diseases.

Along with refining my therapeutic skills, I dove deeper into hypnosis, various imagery techniques and methods from religious, esoteric, spiritual, and magickal traditions. This specialized interest was the result of working with spiritual issues under Father Melton's supervision. I soon found workable imageries I could use with various spiritual concerns. In the Christian Carmelite tradition, I used a structured imagery technique to move into the interior castle to find the divine within. The interior castle is an individual's deep inner spiritual self or soul. This method used graduated guided imagery steps that took my clients as well as myself into the core of our being connecting with the divine within—our eternal soul.

Conversely, other spiritual traditions offered a smorgasbord of methods, but the ones I found most useful allowed me to experiment with out-of-body experiences. I tried a few out-of-body techniques with little success, but the one that worked for me at the time was Bob Monroe's roll out method and later the Hemi-Sync method using binaural sound frequencies. Bob Monroe was the founder of the Monroe Institute which explores altered states of consciousness. Using the roll out method helped me to get out of my body locally. I could see the house I lived in and the community around me from the perspective of looking from above. However, I became dissatisfied with this method because I could not venture into other realities in the hope of getting some insight into my death at birth and where my soul was really from.

Years later, I experimented with Robert Bruce's astral dynamic method, which included a special symbol acting as a portal and it worked. This out-of-body method eventually opened the doorway into a parallel reality in which I found myself overlooking a white city of domes that felt like home. I was able to venture into this parallel reality about five times and then something happened in the last two attempts. I tried to project myself down into the white city of domes and each attempt failed. When I tried the experiment again and several times thereafter, I could not go through the portal into that reality; it appeared I was blocked because the doorway had closed.

Not only did the out-of-body methods yield positive results, but once again I began exploring the world's esoteric and magickal traditions. These traditions offered a variety of meditations and imagery methods, and the one I found most useful was Kabbalistic pathworking, a method I practiced years earlier with effective results. However, with a better understanding of these techniques under my belt, pathworking began yielding detailed images. Magickal pathworking comes from the magickal Kabbalistic tradition and are guided imagery methods that accesses a plethora of imaginary inner worlds within the spheres and paths on the Kabbalistic Tree of Life. Each sphere and path along the Tree of Life is a separate reality replete with landscapes and animated beings. At the time, I had no idea where these realities existed, but later discovered they existed in the imaginal realm.

The imaginal realm was first introduced by Henry Corbin (1972), a scholar of Islamic Studies at the Sorbonne in Paris, France. Corbin translated and interpreted Sufi and Persian texts and discovered there are realities or realms of imagination existing alongside, interpenetrating, and encompassing our physical reality. He labeled this reality the imaginal realm to distinguish it from illusions, fantasies, and hallucinations. The objects and entities existing in this realm are fundamentally different from our everyday imagination. Although different, but similar to dreams, we can see, hear, touch, taste, smell, feel, know, and sense things intellectually, emotionally, and spiritually as if that reality already existed (Duncan, Special Issue, Vol. 10, No. 3).

These imagery traditions, especially Kabbalistic magickal pathworking, allowed me to explore the imaginal realm and later began using variations of these techniques with my clients. One client I had been working with was struggling with deep mental and emotional issues around his body image, extreme masochism and negative feelings surrounding his sexual orientation resulting in a therapeutic impasse. To break the impasse, I decided to create an imagery tailored specifically to his needs. I restructured and refined a variation of the Kabbalistic pathworking imagery, and coupled it with Jung's method of active imagination, creating an imaginary journey, allowing my client mentally to travel deep within his psyche to explore his unconscious. The template I used to create the inner landscape was the cave from Dante's Inferno, and deep within the cave was an archetypal wise woman who could answer my client's questions. I didn't know if the imagery would work, but it was worth a try.

According to Jung, archetypes are part of our collective unconscious and normally are accessed through dreams and imagination. So, to access my client's inner world to connect with the archetypal wise woman, I had him relax to become receptive to the imagery process. Once relaxed, I gently guided him on the inward journey into the imaginary cave deep within his unconscious. In the cave, he met the wise woman and conversed with her. I had instructed my client not to put words into the wise woman's mouth but allow her to speak freely about the questions he needed answered. When I brought him out of the experience, his questions were answered about his body image, extreme masochism, and his negative feelings toward his sexual orientation.

My client had been born with a severe hip joint malformation and was immobilized every night in a brace until he was a teenager, creating an intense loathing toward his body resulting in extreme masochism. Also, as a result of circumcision, his penis retracted up into his body a condition called concealed penis, which made his penis small. Many men are afflicted with this medically created condition resulting from the unnecessary stone age tribal practice of circumcision, which attributes to poor body image and low self-esteem.

Because of the condition of having a small penis, men in the gay community would shun him resulting in negative feelings toward his sexual orientation, which only exacerbated his poor self-image and low self-esteem. The wise woman revealed that these conditions, being immobilized in a brace, negative feelings around his sexual orientation and having a small penis were why he loathed himself and practiced masochistic behaviors. Once the impasse was broken, therapy progressed smoothly.

I later learned the cave in the imagery was called a thoughtform egregore created through imagination. According to Gaetan Delaforge (1988, p. 12) egregores are "created when people consciously come together for a common purpose. Whenever people gather together to do something an egregore is formed, but unless an attempt is made to maintain it … it will dissipate. However, … [if] people wish to maintain it and know the techniques of how to do so, the egregore will continue to grow in strength and can last for centuries. An egregore has the characteristic of having an effectiveness greater than the mere sum of its individual members. It continuously interacts with its members, influencing them and being influenced by them …. If this process is continued a long time the egregore will take on a kind of life of its own and can become so strong that even if all its members should die, it would continue to exist on the inner dimensions [of imaginal realm] …."

Although I had been successful with the imagery in helping my client with his body image and sexual orientation issues, I soon discovered, the imagery didn't work well with women with sexually transmitted diseases. The issue I was having was creating an effective imagery that would reduce the intense shame and guilt around having genital herpes. I knew in order for the imagery to work effectively on these issues, it had to include both hypnosis and behavioral techniques in constructing the imagery. I knew I needed more training using behavioral modalities as well as understanding the psychological impact this disease had on my female clients.

Genital herpes was devastating to my female clients because of how it affected their newborns. It became evident I lacked sufficient training working with sexually transmitted diseases or STDs. To remedy this lack of education and having the knowledge to create a better imagery, in 1984 I began a two-year internship at the Cincinnati Health Department's Sexually Transmitted Disease Clinic.

Within a few months into my internship, one of the male counselors I had been working with informed me the Clinic had just received the first AIDS case in Cincinnati. He asked if I was interested in working on the case with him and I told him I was. Throughout the internship and months following, we worked together on that case as well as other AIDS cases. I became a specialist in HIV and AIDS as well as other sexually transmitted diseases.

Rev. Gary W. Duncan, M.S., M.A., CSM/OCP

Working with HIV and AIDS gave me the opportunity to begin working once again with the terminally ill. At the time, AIDS was a death sentence, and it wasn't long before I began counseling the dying. It soon became evident that several of my clients with AIDS had intense fears surrounding the dying process as well as death and the afterlife. With sufficient training in new therapeutic methods and techniques, as well as a solid foundation in understanding sexually transmitted diseases, I could create a workable imagery to help my clients. My focus shifted from genital herpes to helping people with AIDS go through the dying process. I was able to create an imagery to help relieve their fears and anxieties around dying, death and the afterlife. Because of this new focus and therapeutic demands, I began referring my female clients with genital herpes to other counselors.

The internship provided the therapeutic tools that enable me to create an effective imagery. In conjunction with those tools, I also included various meditations, other imagery techniques such as pathworking, hypnosis, and rituals form a variety of spiritual and esoteric traditions. In designing the imagery, I tapped into other resources as well. I used all my past knowledge and experience with dying, death, the afterlife, the funeral business, working with terminal cancer patients, my academic studies of Kubler-Ross, Anselm Strauss, Ernest Becker, Karlis Osis, and Raymond Moody. However, to round out my knowledge, I reread the Egyptian Book of the Dead and the Tibetan Book of the Dead. I also started attending the local near-death experience group as well as several seminars on dying and death.

The salient population that was the most influential in guiding me into the subtle nuances of how to create the imagery was the personal stories from the near-death-experience group coupled with the Tibetan Book of the Dead's bardo journey. I also felt music along with mindfulness meditation would help my clients settle into a relaxed state. I experimented with various types of music and found the perfect compositions by Marcey Hamm titled "Inward Harmony" (1986). The reason I chose this composition was the way it sounded as well as a profound personal testimonial articulated by a near-death-experiencer. After one of Marcey's concerts, a man came up to her and told her several years ago, he had a heart attack accompanied by a near-death-experience. When he went through the tunnel into the light, the music he heard in the experience was the same as "Inward Harmony".

Working with the dying, the only credential I didn't have was I wasn't a member of the clergy, but that would eventually change. At the time, I had no idea what was in store for me regarding my talents in creating guided imageries for the terminally ill. Working with this population eventually led me to become an ordained Gnostic Catholic Priest as well as a modern-day spiritual psychopomp.

A spiritual psychopomp is a person who escorts or guides the soul on a spiritual journey as well as into the afterlife. In Greek, *psycho* means soul and *pomp* means guide, so a spiritual psychopomp is a guide for the soul. In our modern world, the spiritual psychopomp tradition has changed to not only helping the dying crossover, but also helping people develop their own specific spiritual paths while living.

Chapter 9

UNEXPECTED CONSEQUENCES

ONCE THE IMAGERY WAS IN A WORKABLE FORMAT (SEE APPENDIX A), I begin using it immediately. I had my clients relax on a recliner and guided them into a mindfulness meditation, while Inward Harmony played in the background. Once relaxed, I told them they have two bodies, a physical body, and a soul body. I incorporated the Eastern religious philosophy that at death the soul moves out of the physical body through the seventh chakra at the top of the head. Once the soul was out of the body there waiting were two beings of light. One being of light takes the soul body's right hand and the other being of light takes the left hand. Then the beings of light, escorts the soul body through a dark tunnel toward a dot of light that expands, totally engulfing the soul body. Once in the light, I would leave the soul body there for thirty minutes, and then have the beings of light escort the soul body back into physical reality. Once back, I have the soul body reenter the physical body through the seventh chakra, and then count my clients out of the experience.

Although the imagery was designed to alleviate fears of dying and death, which it did, however, there was an unexpected consequence. At the time, I assumed the imagery was just a made-up drama occurring in the minds of my clients, like other imageries I have used professionally. However, all the clients I used the imagery with had profound mystical experiences when their souls were out of their physical bodies and in the light.

The first client I used the imagery with was Mark and he was in extreme physical pain and going blind, complications from AIDS. He had many fears of dying based on his Roman Catholic upbringing around sin. When I first used the imagery to take Mark's soul body out of his physical body, he became very calm and peaceful. I then allowed the beings of light to guide him gently into the light and left him there for thirty minutes. When I brought him back into his physical body and into ordinary reality, I asked what had happened. He told me he met his sister. I asked, "Your sister who lives in Harrison, Ohio?" He said, "No, my sister that died before I was born." I was startled by his answer.

In a later journey, Mark told me he met his grandmother who raised him and had died several years before. At the time, I couldn't figure out what was happening inside Mark's mind. Mark was slowly going blind, but with these inward journeys into the light, he was becoming calmer, more peaceful and could see his inner world clearly. Mark's experiences were so profound, he asked if I would promise him that when his life-partner James, who also had AIDS, was ready to die, I would take him through the imagery. I promised him I would.

Within a few weeks, Mark was completely blind. He told me the imagery worked so well, were there any methods I knew of that would allow him to see the physical world through a different set of eyes. The only method I came up with was the out-of-body roll-out method pioneered by Robert Monroe at The Monroe Institute. This method I had practiced myself and it worked as well as Monroe's Hemi Sync method. So, over the next several weeks, I taught Mark the roll-out method and he began practicing it with success. He finally related he could see the physical world, but it was very different from anything he had ever experienced. It was so different; he could not find the words to describe it.

Shortly after teaching Mark the roll-out method, he was admitted to the hospital for the last time. As Mark lay dying on the hospital bed, his father told me, Mark came out of a deep sleep and said he could see me and his mother in the room. His father asked the physician about Mark seeing them and was told it was just the morphine, but I knew differently.

I was becoming more baffled with the information Mark was sharing. I just couldn't understand what was happening in the imagery. I was convinced the imagery experience was only occurring in the mind but couldn't explain his unusual stories. I definitely did not think I was actually escorting Mark's soul out of his physical body and into the light, but what was I doing? I was at a loss to explain these unusual stories until I began working with Mark's life-partner James whose experience put it all together for me alongside another strange case I was working with about twin souls merging. All these unusual cases opened many spiritual doorways and by December 1994, I began my seminary journey. It took fifteen years to complete my seminary training, becoming an acolyte, then ordained to the deaconate and finally ordained to the priesthood as a Gnostic Catholic Priest.

James was Roman Catholic and like his life-partner Mark had deep terrifying fears of death and the afterlife because of extreme guilt over being gay and having AIDS. His dying process was extremely painful and fraught with many bouts of denial. At times, he couldn't bring himself to discuss death and had the delusion he would be cured. While working with James, the impact of his experience was so dramatic it changed me, both psychologically and spiritually.

As I watched James deteriorate, it became evident he was running out of time. The promise I had made to Mark kept running through my mind to help James with the imagery when the time came, and the time had come. It took a few months to prepare him for the imagery experience with much resistance on his part. Even discussing the imagery produced extreme anxiety and fear because it signaled his imminent death. However, during the imagery preparation, James was diagnosed with a resistant strain of bacteria that was infecting the frontal lobe of his brain, a complication from AIDS. Within a week after the diagnosis, he was in a semi-comatose condition and placed in a hospice.

I began visiting the hospice weekly along with my life-partner and later my spouse Daryl, who also knew James. During those visits, I was hoping James would become conscious enough so I could take him on the journey into the light. I explained to the hospice nursing staff about the imagery and how it worked, and they were very supportive. On every visit, James's nurse gave me the gloomy prognosis as he slid deeper into a semi-comatose condition. Although semi-comatose, James would lie in bed screaming in pain with his body shaking continuously and not responding to anything said to him. Attempting to address James' uncontrollable shaking and loud outburst, he was given Haldol (Haloperidol) a high potent antipsychotic drug. The drug only exacerbated his semi-comatose condition.

I would stand beside James' bed and talk to him as if he were fully conscious with Daryl standing on the other side of the bed just observing. After leaving the hospice on several occasions, Daryl and I discussed James' condition and his lack of response to any verbal communications. We decided although James was semi-comatose, I should still take him through the imagery experience as promised. James would be the first and only semi-comatose client to experience the imagery and I didn't know if it would work.

The following week, Daryl and I visited James with the intention of taking him through the imagery. James lay in bed shaking and screaming as I began playing the musical composition Inward Harmony. In James' semi-comatose condition, I did not know if he could experience the music, but I continued anyway. As before, Daryl stood on one side of the bed and I on the other.

With music playing in the background, I began talking to James, attempting to guide him into a peaceful meditation as his body continued to shake and he continued to scream. I explained to him, he has a soul body, which is connected to his physical body. Then told him, his soul body is now disconnecting from his physical body and moving toward and through the top of his head. When I told James, his soul body was out of his physical body, his physical body stopped shaking and he went silent. I looked at Daryl and he looked at me with a questioning expression. I shrugged and shook my head indicating I had no idea what was going on—this experience was totally unexpected.

I continued guiding James' soul body through the ceiling and through the next three floors of the hospice facility. On the roof, waiting for James were two beings of light. One took James' right hand and the other took his left hand and escorted him through the darken tunnel into the light. In the light, I told James, he would meet his loved ones who had died—especially Mark; I would leave him with them for thirty minutes and then guide him back.

After thirty minutes, I had the beings of light escort James' soul body back to the hospice roof. I brought James' soul body back down through the three floors. When I told him his soul body was reentering his physical body, he screamed, and his body started shaking again. I as well as Daryl were stunned and emotionally shaken at what we had just witnessed. I had no idea what had taken place inside James's mind.

I had performed the imagery many times and had heard many experiences, but nothing compared to this. At that moment, my worldview shifted and knew

I had experienced something very profound. An insight flooded my awareness; I suddenly knew my decision to enter seminary was sound and I definitely had a spiritual and religious calling. Moreover, I felt the clergy should also be the ones conducting the imagery because as a psychotherapist, I was not trained to work with the mystical experiences unfolding before my eyes.

A week after witnessing the experience with James, I was still trying to grasp the vast implications of the experience when I received a phone call from James' mother informing me, he had died. She requested, I go to the hospice, gather his belongings, and bring them to her. I agreed, went to the hospice and it so happened the nurse who was with James when he died was on duty. Gathering James' belongings, the nurse and I talked about his death. She informed me, she had seen many people die in semi-comatose conditions and many died peaceful, but James' death was different. She said, she watched him for a long time and noticed a subtle comfortableness slowly settling over him as his shaking and vocal outbursts ceased. He became so serene and then he was gone. She indicated it was a beautiful death and attributed it to the imagery.

I continued using the imagery with people who were dying, and they all had similar experiences to those of Mark until I met Phyllis (pseudonym) in a class I was teaching. Unlike Mark, Phyllis was not dying, but in a deep state of grief over the death of her father resulting from a severe long-term illness. Because I was facilitating the imagery in a class format, I had no idea what Phillis was dealing with. I took the class on the inward journey into the light and left them there for thirty minutes. When I brought them back into their physical body and out of the experience, Phillis began crying. I allowed her time to regain composure and asked what had happened. She said she met her father in the light and he had his dog with him. She revealed her mother hated dogs and would not allow her father to have one. Her father kept in his wallet a picture of the breed of dog he loved, and when she met him in the light, the dog in the picture was with him. The experience with her father lifted the severe grief, and she now knew he was in a better place with his canine friend.

I had now used the imagery with clients who were dying, one in a semi-comatose condition and in Phyllis's case in deep grief. Although I had used the imagery with people in the dying process, I had not used it with people in preparation for death long before they died. I started working with Geoff (pseudonym), one of the longest survivors of AIDS. His viral load was non-detectible, and he was living an ordinary life given his condition. Geoff contacted me for spiritual direction with an emphasis on preparing him for his final journey, and it took about a year to prepare him for the imagery experience.

In the preparation process, one major issue Geoff was dealing with concerned his parents, who were now long deceased. Geoff came from a highly dysfunctional alcoholic family. He grew up feeling unloved and rejected by both parents. He knew his farther hated him and was physically abusive. His mother was very critical and condescending; he felt totally rejected and unloved by both. Geoff hated his father for physically abusing him and disliked his mother intensely for constantly telling him how stupid he was. There was a lot of unfinished business between Geoff and his parents.

After working with Geoff in conjunction with his psychiatrist on issues around his parents, and those related to AIDS, he finally felt ready to take the journey into the light. He felt going into the light would forge a sacred path when his earthy journey finally ended. He had no expectations as to what would happen, or what he would see. He just felt he would be closer to God.

I took Geoff on the journey into the light and after thirty minutes brought him back and out of the experience. He sat for several minutes with tears streaming down his face. As usual, I had Kleenex on hand and waited for him to regain composure. Between emotional outbursts, he informed me he met both his father and mother in the light. In the light, Geoff was able to forgive them both; they accepted his forgiveness and told him they regretted how they treated him in life, and they both loved him deeply. As Geoff sat crying, he told me they all hugged each other and all experienced total forgiveness. The imagery experience changed Geoff's feelings toward his parents, and he now knew when he takes his final journey, they will be waiting to welcome him into the light.

I had presented the imagery with individuals who were dying as well as a few groups from the general population and all had profound experiences. However, I began wondering how spiritual and religious groups would experience the imagery. Within a few months, I was asked to present a lecture and a workshop at a local annual spiritual conference. I decided to present a lecture on near-death-experience and reincarnation followed by a workshop on the imagery. The lecture was a packed house and the workshop had seven participants. This was fine with me because the journey into the light with a spiritual population was purely experimental. I had no idea what these spiritual participants would experience if anything.

The workshop was a two-day affair. The first day, I gave a lecture, instructed the small group on how the imagery was to be performed, and ran them through a practice session. It all ended with questions and answers. The group was very lively with two of the women being very talkative and humorous.

The next morning, I took the group through the imagery and after thirty minutes, brought them back. The two women, who had been very talkative the previous day, were now in tears and would not discuss what they had experienced. Although, one of the women did say she met her husband who had died the previous year. The other woman made no comment; she just sat teary-eyed with a glazed stare. There were two participants a man and a woman who decided to share their experience with the group.

The man said his wife was very beautiful in life. She died three years earlier of Alzheimer's. They had a wonderful life together and he stressed they made love all through their marriage until the disease took over. He said when I took him into the light there she was as beautiful as ever. She was so beautiful; he became sexually aroused and wanted to make love with her. Then suddenly realized where he was and decided this was not the appropriate place to make love. He thanked me for uniting them once again.

The woman had a very different experience involving her cat. She said she was so attached to her cat that when it was time for the veterinarian to put it to sleep, she just could not bring herself to be there when it happened. She left the vet's office in tears, leaving her cat alone to its fate. Afterwards, she felt extreme guilt over her reaction, leaving her poor cat to be put to sleep all alone. While in the light, she met her cat, and it forgave her. Meeting her cat once again allowed her to let go of her guilt.

I soon discovered with other participants, meeting pets in the imagery experience appeared to be a common occurrence. In another workshop with a religious group, a woman whose dog began having major health problems went blind, was in extreme pain and finally died. The woman did everything possible to keep the dog alive out of selfish motives. After the dog died, she realized how selfish she had been and became very guilty. In the imagery she met her dog; it was very happy to be where it was and forgave her. She felt very comforted and left the workshop having a sense of closure.

I have taken many people through the imagery experience, and they all have had similar experiences. In all the imageries I have conducted, the common features are being reunited with deceased loved ones, which also includes pets as well as loosing fears surrounding death. Because of this fact, the question I continue asking myself, "Am I actually taking these people's souls out of their bodies and into the light allowing them to meet their loved ones?" So, to answer that question, I took myself through the imagery and had a profound experience.

My experience was totally different form all the other experiences because I did not meet any of my loved ones who had died. Instead, I found myself in the light and in front of a screen of white light with silhouette figures behind it. Then scenes from my troubled youth began unfolding before my eyes on the white screen, addressing questions around being sexually abused that had haunted me for years. The experience was similar to a life-review that near-death experiencer's have, except in my case, it was on as white screen and confined to specific questions. I also knew, if I crossed through the screen of white light, I would not return to my physical body.

As a Spiritual Psychopomp, I find these experiences uplifting; they have given me intimate knowledge into the first stages of the soul's transition into the afterlife. Unlike near-death-experiences, the imagery experience has a more defined focus. With the imagery, participants have profound spiritual experiences reuniting with their loved ones, giving them a sense of closure, knowing the soul continues after death, eliminating fears around dying and death, letting go of grief and knowing that loved ones will be there to welcome them into the light when their earthly journey has ended. Unlike these experiences, my experience was very different; it only focused on answering troubling questions about my youth.

Near-death-experiences shares all the above characteristics as well as connecting with divine beings, visiting one's future self, and visiting other realities to name a few. In addition, people who have had a near-death-experience have died and have been brought back to life; this gives them a unique view into the spiritual landscapes of the afterlife. However, once back in physical reality these populations have a deep understanding of that final journey. Each journey is shaped by the beliefs and life experiences of the journeyer. In all cases I have worked with, after the participants have journeyed into the light there is no fear of death. Knowing this fact gives me solace that I am actually taking their souls into the light.

Chapter 10

Exploring Past-Lives
or Simultaneous Lives

When I was a junior in high school, I learned how to hypnotize. My brother Fred took training in hypnosis, gave me the course materials, and taught me how to hypnotize using several simple techniques. Once I learned the techniques, I began hypnotizing my friends and classmates. This eventually led to hypnotizing people at parties just for fun. I continued using hypnosis as a source of entertainment becoming a party hypnotist. I didn't take hypnosis seriously until I became a psychotherapist.

Shortly after leaving the Episcopal Church and setting up my private practice, I began working with clients who wanted to stop smoking. From reading professional literature, I knew hypnosis could help with smoking secession. So, I began shifting my talents from a party hypnotist by refining my skills through a year-long training in clinical hypnotist from the University of Cincinnati. Once refined, I began using hypnosis clinically not only helping clients stop smoking, but also dealing with other unwanted habits as well.

Within a few years, I began working with abused children as well as adult survivors of abuse through Parents Anonymous, Cincinnati Family Center and other similar organizations. Working with these organizations as a psychotherapist, I became an expert in abuse and sexual abuse in particular. Working with sexual abuse became challenging when trying to uncover early traumatic memories, so I began refining my hypnosis skills once again. I broadened those skills to include hypnotic age regression in which the client is regressed back in time to an earlier age to uncover traumatic memories.

I had been using hypnotic age regression for a couple of years when I began working with a most difficult rape case resulting in Post-Traumatic Stress Disorder (PTSD). The client was in his twenties, and I was helping him work through the trauma of being gang raped by four jocks in high school. One night after a football game, my client was heading for the bus to take him home when four jocks from his swim class confronted him. They coerced him into a deserted wooded area away from prying eyes and demanded he strip nude. The four of them physically forced him to lie face down in mud and held him there while all four took turns anally raping him.

The focus of therapy was helping my client work through frightening flashbacks from the rape as well as intense anger and fear toward his perpetrators. Besides working with those issues, he also wanted to know why he had been singled out and raped, and what had he done that brought him to such a humiliating experience? In trying to find answers to those questions, three specific fears surfaced in the therapeutic process: macho men, water, and authority figures. He assumed his fear of water was because the men who raped him were from his swim class, and his fear of authority figures, he felt may be linked to his father. After working with him for a while on father issues with no progress, it became evident, I needed to use a different approach to uncover those early repressed memories. He had repressed those memories so successfully; I felt that hypnotic age regression might be the key to unlock and open his mental vault, releasing those memories.

After preparing him for hypnotic age regression, I put him into a light hypnotic trance and began regressing him back in time by five-year increments. The regression uncovered repressed memories of two traumatic situations surrounding authority figures. One situation revolved around how his father treated him throughout his life and the other revolved around water and his swim coach.

His father was a very macho man rejecting and humiliating my client throughout his life because he was very soft, didn't play sports and was ridiculed for being a "mommy's boy". Before my client was in his teens, his mother died leaving him with a rejecting and condescending father. As an adult, he finally disclosed he was gay and his father totally rejected him, telling him he always knew he was a "queer" and never had a real son. His rejecting and condescending father created deep fears around authority figures; setting the stage for verbal abuse he would later suffer by his swim coach and classmates.

His fear of authority figures was exacerbated by a terrifying situation in his first year of high school. In swim class, his coach had the class swim nude. My client was afraid to take off his swim-trunks because he was turned on to some of his classmates and felt he might get an erection. Also, his penis had been mangled because of circumcision and he was embarrassed by the way it looked. The swim coach using threats finally succeeded in getting him to swim nude and as expected, his classmates as well as the swim coach made fun of him. On several occasions, he did get an erection and was further humiliated by being called a "fag", setting the stage for later humiliation by being gang raped.

These traumas were so painful, I knew he would never completely work through them. However, being successful at uncovering those hidden traumatic memories inflected by his father, the swim coach, and the four jocks, my client made what I thought at time was an unusual request. He asked if I would regress him to a past life to find out if there were traumatic situations in another lifetime that contributed to him being singled out, raped and humiliated. At the time, I had never performed a past-life regression and told him we had to take a few weeks to prepare for the experience. This was a ploy on my part to give me enough time to research how to use hypnosis for past-life regressions.

I soon discovered there were two major techniques used for past-life regressions: traditional hypnosis, and affect-bridge. With traditional hypnosis, past-life regressions were just an extension of the age regression technique I was already using. Conversely, the affect-bridge technique was similar to hypnotic age regression, except with this technique, one takes an emotion and moves that emotion back in time finding out at what age the emotion was experienced and what events were manifesting around that emotion. The emotion was then moved further back in time, and eventually the emotion moved beyond birth into another lifetime. Since I was already using hypnotic age regression, I decided to continue using that technique rather than affect bridge.

After a light hypnotic induction, I began counting my client back in time by five-year increments. When I got to his birth, I continued counting him back before he was born. My client had been born in the late 1960s, so when I counted him back to the 1940s, he told me to stop because something was happening. He said he was in the water and having difficulty swimming because there were objects whizzing through the water at him. He then revealed the objects were bullets, and he was being shot at. He then said, "I'm wearing an American Army uniform. It's D-Day and I'm shot—I'm sinking—I'm shot again—I'm dying. I can see above my body—a lot of solders are getting killed. I can see them separating from their bodies. I'm moving and I don't know where I'm going." At that moment, I was feeling very uneasy with what I was hearing, so decided to count him out of the experience. When I brought him back, he was shaken and so was I.

It took several months to process my client's past-life experience as being a soldier in the D-Day invasion. He slowly began to understand why he had so many fears surrounding water, authority figures and humiliation. He concluded his fears around water were because he was killed in the water during the D-Day invasion. His fears with authority figures were centered on being ordered to sacrifice his life in the invasion—he simply had no choice in the matter. I found his conclusion regarding humiliation interesting because he felt shamed by not living long enough to have an impact on the invasion by killing some German soldiers.

Knowing he was once a soldier in a very important military campaign gave him the strength to deal with his perpetrators. Years later, on two separate occasions, he saw two of the men who had raped him. On one occasion, he saw one of the men with his family eating at a restaurant. On the other occasion, he saw one of the other men with his wife eating at another restaurant. Both times, he would sit at his table and just stare at the rapist making them feel very uncomfortable. My client knew the rapist didn't want their families, especially their wives, to know their husbands raped men. The men quickly finished eating and swiftly left the restaurants. It gave my client comfort to know he was controlling their movements as well as knowing their unsavory hidden secret.

After conducting several past-life regressions with success, I was becoming more comfortable with the process. It became evident these past-life stories were having a therapeutic impact on my clients by helping them uncover past-life traumas that were affecting current lifetime. By this time, conducting past-live regressions was dovetailing with the imagery work I was also doing with the terminally ill. Both past-life regressions and the imagery experiences were giving me two pieces of a gigantic afterlife puzzle that may offer some insight in my own death at birth.

I was also discovering past-life regressions were unveiling problematic memories from another lifetime that were remarkably similar to the struggles my clients were having in their current lifetime. However, I began questioning are past life stories actually true or are they memory fragments cobbled together to create an allegorical narrative to deal with a current situation. I knew with hypnosis that hidden or forgotten memories could be reconstructed to create a story that never took place a phenomenon called cryptomnesia. "Cryptomnesia occurs when a forgotten memory returns without its being recognized as such by the subject, who believes it is something new and original. It is a memory bias whereby a person may falsely recall generating a thought, an idea, a tune, a name, or a joke, not deliberately engaging in plagiarism but rather experiencing a memory as if it were a new inspiration" (Wikipedia).

Working with those past-life or cryptomnesia memories was having a positive therapeutic effect helping my clients resolve their current issues. They were gaining new insights into unfinished business from a possible created previous lifetime that was affecting their current situations. This enabled them to defuse and release the emotional residue by re-working and cutting the ties to those created past-life situations, which resulted in profound psychological healing.

The imagery experiences and the past-life regressions were both having profound healing effects on my clients. The imagery experiences primarily involved working with deceased loved ones around unfinished business as well as giving my clients a snapshot into the experience of being in the light. Conversely, past-life regressions were specifically focused on possible created past-life memories that were affecting my client's current lifetime. The results of both experiences were helping my clients move into a healthier emotional state.

With the imagery experience, I had a partial understanding how the process worked because I took myself through the imagery. However, with past-life regressions I had very little understanding of what was actually going on in the experiences, so I decided to take myself through the experience. It took a few years to find the exact method that would allow me to uncover my past-lives and gain an understanding of how cryptomnesia worked. In 1988, a colleague and I decide to take a highly recommended course through Edgar Cayce's, Association for Research and Enlightenment called "How to Discover Your Past Lives".

At first, when I started the course, I was very skeptical of the technique because it was different from the regression technique, I was using but I was soon surprised by the outcome. Unlike the past-life regression technique I was using with clients, this course used audio tapes to help regress me. The course also included a workbook that allowed me to explore my connections with various historical lifetimes activating my cryptomnesia response. Initially nothing happened, but I continued to trudge through the course. Finally, the dam broke, and possible cryptomnesia scenes began to flood into my inner awareness laying out four distinct past-life scenarios in vivid detail. In all four scenarios, my experience was male; I have no conscious recollections, connections, insights, or feelings of experiencing being a female in any of those lifetimes.

What surprised me the most was how the past-life scenarios took shape. In all four scenarios, I was looking through another man's eyes, seeing what he saw. I never had the experience that it was actually me looking through the eyes as being that person but only me looking through someone else's eyes. Being in that person's body, I could see the scenes vividly through his eyes, feel how he felt emotionally, hear the conversations taking place, detect objects by touch, could smell the varied scents and experience what was being thought—it was as though I was there but in another man's body.

Over the next several months, these four past-life scenarios would unfold, following a historical sequence beginning I assumed in the 1300s and ending in the 1940s. In the first past-life scenario, which was quite lengthy, I was looking through the eyes of a monk in the Middle Ages. He was wearing a monk's whitish-gray colored robe with a black scapular with hood; the monastic order was Dominican. He was an educator and appeared to have influence because he had a young novice as his assistant. The young novice was also in a sexual relationship with the monk, which was not uncommon for that period, but was against monastic rules. Although he was a teacher of theology, the monk and his novice were experimenting with secret books of magick.

The monastery was on a plateau high above a river that meandered through the valley below. The languages spoken in the monastery were Latin, French, and Italian. There were other monastic orders present as well because some monks wore black robes signifying, they were Benediction, and some monks wore brown robes signifying they were Franciscan.

As I was experiencing the rapid changing scenes in the past-life scenario, I became a separate observer of the scenes, and at other times I was peering through the eyes of the monk and could experience his inner thoughts. In one scene as the observer, I was watching the monk and his assistant perform a magickal ritual. Shortly thereafter, the monk and his assistant were caught practicing magick and brought before the Abbot. The monk knew the Abbot's hidden secret that he was sexually turned-on to very young boys. The Abbot knowing the monk knew this fact decided rather than bringing the monk and his novice to trial for heresy, he would kick them out of the monastery to prevent his own disclosure.

The monk and his assistant left the monastery, crossing the river below. They found a small abandon stone fort-like structure down river from the monastery and settled in. Once settled, they continued experimenting with magick with the intentions of changing the world in a positive direction by cultivating compassion and love in a world that was devoid of such acts. Most of the magickal rituals focused on abstaining from sex before the rituals were performed, however, with some rituals the monk and his assistant conducted sex magick. In these rituals, sexual energy was used in an attempt to attain compassion and love.

In one scene, the assistant was still nude after a sex ritual. He was sitting beside the monk who was half-clad looking out a gray stone glassless window. Suddenly, my awareness shifted and rather looking at the scene as an observer, I was looking out the window through the eyes of the monk, seeing the beautiful greenery all around. I could see across the river and up the steep hillside to where the monastery sat on the plateau. Being inside the monk, I was privy to his inner thoughts. He was in deep contemplation about how he never fit in with a monastic lifestyle and felt totally out of place in a cruel and uncaring world. The scenes and details in this past-life scenario unfolded over a period of several weeks.

A few months later, the second past-life drama unfolded; I was looking through the eyes of a Spanish conquistador conquering the Aztecs and other Native tribes. In this drama, the conquistador was helping Catholic friars force Native people to convert to Christianity. The scene was one of mass killings in which, the conquistadors were killing men and women by cutting off one foot at a time and throwing them over a cliff until the tribe converted.

The scene was very bloody; I could smell the musty, rancid sickening odor of the conquistador sweat mixed with putrid smells of blood and flesh. Blood was splattered all over his uniform. I became the observer and saw the conquistador stop for a few minutes to take off his helmet and wipe the sweat from his forehead and matted hair. The scene rapidly changed, and I was looking through his eyes again. He was on horseback chasing a female Native as he sliced off her head. Years later, a female client in a past-life regression had a possible cryptomnesia memory of a similar scene. She saw herself running from a conquistador on horseback. She said, I was the conquistador, and I was wearing a uniform replete with helmet and drawn sword. I rode up beside her and sliced off her head. This client felt we came back together in this lifetime to work through that tragic event.

The next past-life scenario was very short; I was looking through the eyes of a taskmaster in the slave fields in the Old South. In this past-life scenario, the scene opens with me as the observer looking at a man standing with one foot on the lower step of a white pillared porch of a southern colonial planta-tion house. The man was wearing a red plaid flannel-type shirt, brown dirty pants with a coiled whip on the right side attached to a hook and brown muddy boots. Then suddenly my perspective shifted, I was looking through the eyes of the taskmaster, looking up and talking to a bearded man standing on the porch wearing a white suite, who owned the plantation. The conversation was about the field slaves, and then the scene changed, to me looking through his eyes at the slaves working the field as sexual thoughts run through his mind.

He looked at one of the slaves, a black man with whom he was having sex. He was not only a field slave, but a sex slave as well.

This past-life scenario was interesting because years later it came up in a psychotherapy session while working with the strange case of twin soul's merging of Jean Cline and George Reeves. I regressed Jean to a past life in the Old South where she was the wife of George living on their plantation. In this past-life regression, George began talking through Jean about a past-life he and I lived during that period. At the time, Jean and George knew nothing about me having a past-life experience as taskmaster in the Old South. George began telling me he and I grew up together and were childhood friends and at times, our friendship became sexual. His family owned the plantation next to the one I worked on, in which I was a taskmaster to the field slaves. His confirmation of that past life was startling to say the least.

However, the past-life experienced as the taskmaster was not me, but it was me looking through the eyes of the man who was the taskmaster. What I assumed was going on with George was he was telepathically connecting with my possible cryptomnesia memories, finding the past-life story, and used it to his advantage. He created a story about he and I in the Old South being friends and living on neighboring plantations trying to make a connection with me, but I remained skeptical. I had very little trust in him and didn't like him at all because I felt he was possessing Jean. I later concluded Jean was also possessing George; she wanted him to be a part of her—a case of dual possession. Because of the dual possession, Jean was transforming physically looking like George; this is not a twin soul but only a dual possession.

The last past-life scenario took me over two decades to understand its ramifications. This past-life scenario occurred at Auschwitz, the Nazi extermination camp. In the first scene, I am looking through the eyes of a physician named Hans Kruger making selections. A woman was standing before him with a brown headscarf pulled tight around her head and tied under the chin. Her brown eyes were very sad, and her face was dirty. I could see his black leathered gloved right hand with extended index finger pointing at her and his thump directs her to the left indicating she was to become slave labor and would not at that time go to the gas chamber.

The scene rapidly changed; I was no longer looking through the eyes of the Nazi perpetrator, but now looking through the eyes of a victim. He was a gay prisoner wearing a pink triangle and slowly dying of typhus. I was now the observer and could see the victim dead and his body was being shoved into a crematorium. I could see his body consumed in flame. This unusual past-life scenario allowed me to experience what it was like observing both a perpetrator as well as a victim.

After experiencing these four past-life scenarios, I continued to explore past-lives, but in the following decades could not retrieve any more past-life experiences. I continued trying to find past-lives situations that occurred before the 1300s and found nothing. It's as though these four past lives were the only ones I was associated with, by way of possible cryptomnesia. In all four scenarios, my experience was male and in three I was same gender oriented—a monk, taskmaster and the prisoner in Auschwitz.

In the first past-life of the monk, he was caught in an oppressive abusive religious system. However, within that system the monk and his assistant were trying to make the world a better place through magick. In the second, third and fourth past-life scenarios the conquistador, the taskmaster and the Nazi perpetrator, were caught in an oppressive abusive system using their power to inflict pain and suffering. However, in the fourth past-life still caught in an oppressive abusive system, I experienced what it was like being inside the bodies of both a perpetrator and a victim. It was as though, I came into this reality to experience the world through the eyes of the monk, which had good intentions, but as the conquistador, the taskmaster and Nazi perpetrator, I experienced what it was like being a tyrant inflicting much pain. Conversely, in the last past-life scenario, my two experiences were balanced in knowing what it felt like being inside the bodies of both a perpetrator and a victim. In all four scenarios, the past-life characters were caught in an oppressive religious or political system.

After experiencing these four past-life scenarios from the course "How to Discover Your Past Lives", I concluded the hypnotic regression tapes put me in a state of high suggestibility, which is what happens under hypnosis. Being highly suggestible allowed my mind to possibly create those experiences from forgotten memories because as a history buff, I could easily create these scenarios unconsciously by cobbling them together into a past-life mosaic. It is evident my mind picked different forgotten memory fragment and created an experience that was relevant to the situation I was currently experiencing. This suggestibility factor could be relevant with the client who experienced being in the D-Day invasion. He too could have cobbled together fragments from his forgotten memories as well as conscious memories to create a past live that reflected his current situation.

Over the years, I had read a vast amount of material on past lives, reincarnation, as well as karma. I have always had problems with both past lives and reincarnation and after experiencing my own past-life scenarios I now know why. In all these experiences, I was not the characters in the past lives but an observer looking through their eyes or an observer looking from a different position, all a made-up drama representing a current struggle.

As I assessed my experiences as well as the client with the D-Day invasion scenario some questions came to mind. In my case, why was I not the person in those experiences? Because those experiences are not real past lives but made up from forgotten memories that represents a current situation. Also, could past-life experiences come from our collective unconscious enabling us to connect with someone's experiences in a parallel or simultaneous reality? This could be another way we create past-life sceneries by connecting with stories that already exist in our collective unconscious, which is packed with all kinds of experiences. Because of our own situation we connect with someone else's historical experience in the collective unconscious to help resolve our current struggles. These are not past lives at all, but situations stored in our collective unconscious or thoughts from people or beings we are connecting with existing in some other reality all stored in our collective unconscious. Or could be just cryptomnesia stories coupled with experiences from parallel realities.

Chapter 11

REINCARNATION AND KARMA

MY SKEPTICISM AS WELL AS INTEREST IN REINCARNATION AND KARMA began in the late 1960s, when I read Morey Bernstein's book *The Search for Bridey Murphy*. This reincarnation case not only intrigued me, but also laid out three basic questions, "Have I lived before?" If so, "Who was I, and what were those lifetimes like?" These three questions ignited an intense literature search that brought me to Joseph Head and Sylvia Cranston's seminal work, *Reincarnation: The Phoenix Fire Mystery* (1977/1991). This work looked at reincarnation from a cultural, philosophical, psychological, and historical perspective. When I originally read the book in the late 1970s, I gained a basic understanding of reincarnation and karma. These two books eventually led to the work of Helena P. Blavatsky, one of the founders of Theosophy, who introduced the doctrine of reincarnation and karma to the West in the late 1800s.

During that time, Blavatsky's views were shaped mostly by Hinduism with a little mixture of Buddhism in which the doctrine of reincarnation was organized and shaped by karma. Karma means actions, whether those actions are positive or negative. These actions shape the reincarnation process from lifetime to lifetime until those actions are addressed. Once addressed, the soul is released from the cycle of samsara (pain and suffering), or continual death and rebirth, allowing the soul to move into a better lifetime or repeat the process all over again. In some cases, karma was so severe the soul incarnated into a lower form of animal, a process known as metempsychosis. With metempsychosis, the soul begins the incarnational journey from a lower form of animal progressing to a higher form of animal and eventually into human, or from a human into a lower form of animal, depending on one's karmic debt (Richelieu, 1958/1989).

Until Blavatsky began exporting the doctrine of reincarnation and karma into the Western world, the concept of karma was absent in most discourse. Not only was karma absent, but reincarnation was limited just to metempsychosis. The prevailing book at the time that discussed reincarnation was Thomas Jay Hudson's *The Law of Psychic Phenomena*. In this work, reincarnation was simply a form of metempsychosis in which the soul evolves from lower forms of animals through a succession of reincarnations into the pinnacle of existence—the human. According to William L. Reese (1996, p. 478), metempsychosis is a salient feature in the reincarnation doctrines of Hinduism, Jainism and Mahayana Buddhism.

However, Blavatsky had a very different take on reincarnation and karma because she reinterpreted these concepts to fit within the Western religious traditions eliminating metempsychosis altogether. In her book, *Isis Unveiled* (1972/1997, p. 87), karma became another word for sin. Blavatsky states karma is "the law of cause and effect as applied to an individual's moral life." For her, it was a fixed law of retribution like the Christian concept of sin in that this law is expressed in the cycle of death and rebirth (samsara) in which an individual's actions come back on them through rewards and punishments as in Hinduism and Buddhism. In this view, karma not only occurs in one's present life, but also continues into their next life. Blavatsky (1972/1997, p. 87) further states, "… the present life and circumstances of an individual are the result of his [or her] deeds and thoughts in past lives." She was adamant in not believing "that humans can reincarnate again as animals." She felt the reincarnated soul re-embodies itself on the earth plane in human form until it overcomes "all the forces that tie it to this planet".

The fundamental doctrine of metempsychosis in which humans incarnate into animals or animals incarnate into humans has never been accepted in Western cultures. Within the Western context, reincarnation through karmic effects is an evolutionary progression from lower evolved humans into higher evolved humans, which is unlike metempsychosis, a process of de-evolutionary regression—from humans into animals.

According to Jane Bletzer (1987, p. 531), this evolutionary progression is based on the belief that "the life force of the physical body does not die with the physical body but goes on living in the" world of the spirit "for a period of time". It is then reincarnated back on earth once again, "repeating this hundreds of times until the life force has perfected itself." This perfection of the life force through progressive reincarnational cycles is another way of understanding karma.

Similarly, according to Nicolas Goodrick-Clark (2004, p. 16), Blavatsky's understanding of karma simply means the law of cause and effect as applied to an individual's moral life. Within this context, Blavatsky makes distinctions between moral causes and instrumental causes. She states, "like the revolutions of a wheel, there is a regular succession of death and birth, the moral cause of which is the cleaving to existing objects" (attachments), "while the instrumental cause is karma," which is the power that "controls the universe … [resulting in the qualities of] … merit and demerit" (1972/1997, p. 87) all centered around one's actions.

Although Blavatsky eliminated metempsychosis and Christianized karma as merit and demerit by equating it with sin, however, sin and karma have very different meanings. The original meaning of sin is from the Greek word 'hamartia' meaning, "missing the mark", in reference to an archery target, in which the arrow misses the bull's eye. Over the centuries, Christianity has changed the meaning of sin to fit within its changing theology. Sin from this perspective is any grievous act a person commits, which dooms him or her to an eternal existence in hell, but not through cycles of reincarnation. Conversely, Blavatsky's view of karma, is, rather than an existence in hell, the sinner is doomed to repeat their seeds of destruction, lifetime after lifetime until they work through those negative actions. In other words, the bad deeds one sowed in the last lifetime will plague them in the present lifetime, until they change those actions to perfect their soul's life force. Once karma is worked through and life force is perfected, the soul is reborn (not reincarnated) into higher states of consciousness.

If Blavatsky really believed what she was writing and saying about karma, then why did she abuse her power by performing devious and charlatan acts? She lied about her journey to Tibet—there are no records she was ever there. In her séances, she deceived people by pretending to call various spirits fooling people by performing elaborate hoaxes—bottom line she did have some psychic abilities but in the big picture she was a charlatan. Not only was she a charlatan but her history indicated she was an ardent racist as well. If she really believed in karma, she would not have been a racist con artist.

Blavatsky was not alone in equating karma with sin. The Indiana yogi Paramahansa Yogananda had a similar viewpoint when he introduced kryra-yoga to the West, years later. Kryra-yoga comes from the same Sanskrit root as karma meaning to do, to act, or react. Yogananda's interpretation of karma (1946/2001; 1982/2008, p. 434) is an equilibrating law in which it manifests in action and reaction, cause and effect and sowing and reaping. "In the course of natural righteousness, every human being by his [or her] thoughts and actions becomes the molder of their own destiny. Whatever energies he [or her], wisely or unwisely, has set in motion must return to him [or her] as their starting point, like a circle inexorably completing itself …. A person's karma follows him [or her] from incarnation to incarnation until fulfilled or spiritually transcended".

Yogananda further states in a broader context that karma is also "the cumulative actions of human beings within communities, nations, or the [entire] world, [which] constitutes mass karma, produc[ing] local or far-ranging effects according to the degree and preponderance of good or evil. The thoughts and actions of every human being, therefore, contribute to the good or ill of this world and all peoples in it" (1946/2001; 1982/2008, p. 434).

If Yogananda really believed this, then his sexual exploitations and indiscretions with female devotees would have doomed him in his current incarnation as well as future reincarnations. Since it appears he did not suffer at all in this lifetime for his sexual exploitation of women; the question then becomes, what is karma and does it really exist. If spiritual figures such as Blavatsky and Yogananda as well as other spiritual leaders does bad deeds and does not suffer for it, then what does all this mean, I began asking myself. At this point, I began researching karma from a different perspective.

Blavatsky and Yogananda's views of reincarnation hold that through karma one is doomed to an existence in hell, or doomed to repeat their actions, lifetime after lifetime. However, I soon discovered there was a very different view of karma and reincarnation that emerged alongside Blavatsky and Yogananda's teachings. This view came from the Indian yogi Sri Aurobindo. His understanding of karma was not an unyielding or fixed state, but a more fluid state based on free will. To paraphrase Aurobindo (1952/1991, p. 69), karma uses "universal Energy", or life force to set in motion a "process of actions" that assembles and disassembles things. This process is a continuous chain of events in which causes and effects, govern each separate link in the chain. Present actions are the product of past actions and future actions is the product of present actions.

Aurobindo used karmic actions to change his life into the direction he desired. Karma from this standpoint is an evolutionary progression in which free will plays a central role in shaping one's reality. Aurobindo (1993/2007, pp. 343-347) indicated that spiritual evolution of the soul, governed by free will enables the individual to evolve within each lifetime as he or she chooses. In essence, individuals are not slaves to karma, but karma presents opportunities to evolve spiritually. To me this is simply the power of using free will in the form of thoughts, visualization, and intention to create a new life to be reborn into and has nothing to do with the traditional meaning of karma. From this perspective, it appears karma is just a form of free will produced by our conscious and unconscious thoughts, actions, and intentions.

However, the part of Aurobindo's philosophy that was most liberating is the fact we have free will within the processes of karma, and that free will liberate us from past actions. He states, "I am a soul developing and persisting in the paths of the universal Energy and that ... is the seed of ... my [own] creation." He further indicates that what he has become was achieved through the will power of his soul's past ideas and actions, which also affected his present and future ideas and action (Aurobindo, 1952/1991, p. 74).

In shaping the soul's destiny, karmic will power plays a major role influencing one's reincarnation experiences. Aurobindo puts a slight twist on the concept of reincarnation and uses rebirth instead. In this view, the soul goes through the process of evolution directed by the force of karmic free will, which is unlike the traditional understanding of reincarnation, where free will is absent. He states, "the perception of rebirth ... for ... spiritual evolution ... makes life a significant [spiritual] ascension and not a mechanical ... [process]; it opens to us the divine vistas of a growing soul; it makes the world a nexus of spiritual self-expansion; it sets us seeking ... for the self-knowledge of our spirit and the self-fulfillment of a wise and divine ... existence" (Aurobindo, 1952/1991, p. 38). "Once we find that there is a conscious Spirit [in the reincarnation process] ... we are bound... to grow... [in] that new ... evolution ...

striving to be delivered … [into a] … greater birth ….” This new “birth … must be … in harmony with the intention of the Spirit … and not … spiritual incoherencies and contradictions” (Aurobindo, 1952/1991, p. 45-46).

According to Aurobindo, “there comes a time when the soul becomes aware of itself … then aware of the … present,” and “sees how … [the] past, remembers something of [its] … soul-states, and … activity which [has] built up its present constituents” … [in developing a future]. “This is the true dynamic … of rebirth, and there too [our questioning intellect ceases, resulting in our] soul’s vision and … memory [is] all that exist” (Aurobindo, 1952/1991, p. 11). I would add that rebirths are not only future incarnations but a rebirth in one’s present lifetime is spiritual awakening, a form of ascension.

Aurobindo’s concept of rebirth also takes on a broader perspective when he uses the concept of ‘ascension’. Ascension indicates one is reborn into higher states of consciousness, which can be in any reality or realm. In this context, rebirth is similar to the Buddhist doctrine of metempsychosis in which a person’s soul is not always reborn as another human being but can be reborn into one of six realms or realities. This indicates the soul can be reborn into any simultaneous realty. Based on Aurobindo’s beliefs this can be achieved through free will, directing our soul to be reborn into any reality we chose (Matthews, 1986, pp.123-144). Bottom line, reincarnation is the soul coming back to the earth plane over and over again. Whereas rebirth is ascending into higher states of consciousness or reborn into other realms and realities.

Aurobindo used karma in the evolutionary process to reshape his destiny through will power. He used actions and reactions to mold his soul into the perfection he desired. And this perfection can be ascending into higher states of consciousness as well as being reborn into other realms or realities. This legacy of reshaping one’s future through will power is currently part of modern yogic practices.

According to Linda Johnsen (2012, p. 10), if a person desires to use karma to change their destiny “[they] need to think seriously about what [they] want from life, where [they] want to go, and what [they] want to achieve. If [you’re] not happy with the direction [you’re] going in, [you] need to begin working consciously with the force of [your] karma. Then [you] can redirect the flow of [your] destiny, rather than passively allowing it to carry [you] away.” Again, this author is talking about will power. Is will power just another name for karma, and not connected to the act of retribution in the moral sense.

The changing of one's destiny through will power in reincarnation or rebirth is also present in Tibetan Buddhist visualization and meditation practices. A group of high-ranking lamas called tulkus practice visualization and meditation techniques to change their next incarnation into the outcome they desire. According to Alexandra David-Neel (1932, p. 117; 1997, pp. 87), this group of tulkus reject the Buddhist doctrine that denies the existence of the soul as well as the permanent ego. They believe the early Buddhist made a grave error in this regard by not accepting the Hindu doctrine of the self or jiva. In this belief jiva or self undergoes periodic changes in which the old warn out body is exchanged for a new one through will power and intention. These tulkus use will power in a similar manner as Aurobindo in shaping their next incarnation.

According to David-Neel (1932, p. 118; 1997, pp. 87), this group of tulkus believe in the existence of the self and the transmigration of the self from one incarnation into the next incarnation. These tulkus have strong personalities in that they can remember their previous lifetimes and "at the time of death" are able "to choose and make known the place of their next birth and their future parents". In other words, tulkus' can change and shape their next lifetime by choosing their parents, so they can have a specific personality, living a specific life, having specific experiences they desire.

Karma or actions are an integral part of the traditional reincarnation process as discussed by Blavatsky, Yogananda, Aurobindo and the Tibetan Buddhist tulkus. Within this doctrine they believe after death their souls move on into the next afterlife and after working through karmic issues, they reincarnate back into the material world. This is like the Tibetan Bardo's in-between state journey in which the soul goes through a 49-day afterlife journey and then incarnates back into physical form (Evans-Wentz, 1975; Thondup, 2006; Padmasambhave, 2006).

Jane Bletzer's (1987, p. 531) explanation of reincarnation is based on a similar belief that "there is a human being seed encased within the soul-mind of every individual that contains the essence of perfection... This seed declares that the soul-mind of an individual cannot and does not attain perfection in one earth life[time] but requires many cycles of experiences in" the earth "plane." For the evolution of reincarnation to continue "the soul-mind assumes a succession of personalities ... [that are] born into ... different ... periods of history, different cultures ... and different amounts of wealth, all carrying many kinds of [karmic] emotional and intellectual experiences" until the soul-mind is perfected. In essence, once the soul-mind has reached perfection it will reincarnate into the next earthly lifetime. The question I began asking about Bletzar's explanations is, does she have any evidence to back up her conclusions about reincarnation or is she just making it all up? I see many holes in her metaphysical explanation as well as those of Blavatsky, Yogananda and Aurobindo.

Like the Tibetan tulkus on their 49-day Bardo in-between state journey Bletzer (1987, p. 531), further explains that "the soul-mind lives many years in-between incarnation[al] states ...." There are past-life regression experiences that support this viewpoint. Subjects have been regressed to the in-between state, just before birth and their next lifetime. According to these regression subjects, their souls in the in-between state chose specific parents to have a particular lifetime experience, similar to the Tibetan Tulkus (Newton, 1996; Wambach, 1981). However, are these in-between states just another form of cryptomnesia or false memories.

Setting cryptomnesia aside, it appears that the traditional understanding of karma does not exist because the soul in the in-between state choose to incarnate to specific parents to have a specific experience. This perspective also rejects the traditional understanding of reincarnation, which is tied to karma in which the soul is reincarnated over and over until karma is worked through. If the soul decides before birth to be born to specific parents, then we are talking about free will and not traditional karma. So, if the soul does not come back to the earth plane but choses to be born into some other reality or realm this is not reincarnation but a form of rebirth. Conversely, if the soul choses to come back to the earth plane whether through karma or free will this is a form of reincarnation. Rebirth occurs with the ascension process as well as being born into other realms and realities. Reincarnation only occurs when the soul is born back into the earth plane.

Souls in the in-between state chose their parents and the lifetime experiences they desire to have, if this is factual, are there any reincarnation cases that backs this up? It took several years researching the work of both Ian Stevenson and Jim Tucker at the University of Virginia's Division of Personality Studies to find a case suggesting we do choose our next lifetime in the in-between state. Child psychiatrist Jim Tucker presented a convincing case that we do create out next lifetime by choosing our parents to have a particular lifetime experience. What makes this case so interesting is it did not occur in the Hindu or Buddhist cultures that believe in reincarnation, but in New York City. Tucker (2005, pp.1-3) presents the case in vivid detail, laying out a scenario that leaves one in awe. The case that follows is in Tucker's own words.

> John McConnell, a retired New York City policeman working as a security guard, stopped at an electronics store after work one night in 1992. He saw two men robbing the store and pulled out his pistol. Another thief behind a counter began shooting at him. John tried to shoot back, and even after he fell, he got up and shot again. He was hit six times. One of the bullets entered his back and sliced through his left lung, his heart, and the main pulmonary artery, the blood vessel that takes blood from the right side of the heart to the lungs to receive oxygen. He was rushed to the hospital but did not survive.

> John had been close to his family and had frequently told one of his daughters, Doreen, "No matter what, I'm always going to take care of you." Five years after John died, Doreen gave birth to a son named William. William began passing out soon after he was born. Doctors diagnosed him with a condition called pulmonary valve atresia, in which the valve of the pulmonary artery has not adequately formed, so blood cannot travel through it to the lungs. In addition, one of the chambers of his heart, the right ventricle, had not formed properly as a result of the problem with the valve. He underwent several surgeries. Although he will need to take medication indefinitely, he has done quite well.

> William had birth defects that were very similar to the fatal wounds suffered by his grandfather. In addition, when he became old enough to talk, he began talking about his grandfather's life. One day when he was three years old, his mother

was at home trying to work in her study when William kept acting up. Finally, she told him, "Sit down, or I'm going to spank you." William replied, "Mom, when you were a little girl and I was your daddy, you were bad a lot of times, and I never hit you!"

His mother was initially taken aback by this. As William talked more about the life of his grandfather, she began to feel comforted by the idea that her father had returned. William talked about being his grandfather a number of times and discussed his death. He told his mother that several people were shooting during the incident when he was killed, and he asked a lot of questions about it.

One time, he said to his mother, "When you were a little girl and I was your daddy, what was my cat's name?"

She responded, "You mean Maniac?"

"No, not that one," William answered. "The white one."

"Boston?" his mom asked.

"Yeah," William responded. "I used to call him Boss, right?"

That was correct. The family had two cats, named Maniac and Boston, and only John referred to the white one as Boss.

One day, Doreen asked William if he remembered anything about the time before he was born. He said that he died on Thursday and went to heaven. He said that he saw animals there and also talked to God. He said, "I told God I was ready to come back, and I got born on Tuesday." Doreen was amazed that William mentioned days since he did not even know his days of the week without prompting. She tested him by saying, "So, you were born on a Thursday and died on Tuesday?" He quickly responded, "No, I died Thursday at night and was born Tuesday in the morning." He was correct on both counts—John died on a Thursday, and William was born on a Tuesday five years later.

He talked about the period between lives at other times. He told his mother, "When you die, you don't go right to heaven. You go to different levels—here, then here, then here" as he moved his hand up each time. He said that animals are reborn as well as humans and that the animals he saw in heaven did not bite or scratch.

John had been a practicing Roman Catholic, but he believed in reincarnation and said that he would take care of animals in his next life. His grandson, William, says that he will be an animal doctor and will take care of large animals at a zoo.

William reminds Doreen of her father in several ways. He loves books, as his grandfather did. When they visit William's grandmother, he can spend hours looking at books in John's study, duplicating his grandfather's behavior from years before. William, like his grandfather, is good at putting things together and can be a "nonstop talker."

William especially reminds Doreen of her father when he tells her, "Don't worry, Mom. I'll take care of you."

What is intriguing about this case is how a soul in the in-between state sculpted their next lifetime through will power. It appears John chose his daughter to be born back in this physical world to take care of her as he promised, and most probably there are other reasons as well. This is not reincarnation coupled with karma, but the free will decision of John's soul. It also appears this basic act of will power allowed his soul in the in-between state to shape his next lifetime by choosing his daughter as his reincarnation medium. What was surprising is when John reincarnated back into physical reality through his grandson William, he brought with him the results of his fatal wounds, which created William's heart condition. Why would John want to inflict such a chronic heart condition on his grandson or his reincarnational self? Is it just to prove his soul is back in physical form and to prove the soul is a reality that can maneuver itself through many lifetime experiences? These questions remain unanswered.

Through William, John tells his daughter that in the in-between state, he existed on many levels of reality and conversed with the divine. Being in many levels of reality is like experiences people have not only in past-life regressions, but also with near-death experiences (Atwater (2007, Newton, 1996; Wambach, 1981). Talking with the divine or God in the afterlife occurs mostly in Western near-death experience cases. However, in Eastern experiences rather than talking with God, they have apparitions of those who have died as well as communicating with religious figures (Osis, 1979). It appears this experience of talking with God or religious figures is shaped by the religion and culture the individual is born into, and John was Roman Catholic. With these cases as well as others, I began doubting the truth of traditional reincarnation and karma. In most cases, they both traditionally seemed to revolve around retribution, which I find not spiritual, but the human belief in revenge.

I also began to entertain what is called reincarnation in which the soul goes through earthly lifetime after earthly lifetime is not valid when connected with karma. The reason I began considering this idea is that if everything that exist is happening in the here and now as most wisdom traditions and quantum physics espouse, then what is called consecutive lifetimes as in reincarnation does not exist. Not only are consecutive lifetimes a ruse but everything is interconnected within simultaneous lifetimes, existing side by side or all at once and not consecutive lifetimes because everything is happening in the present and not a linear progression. What we call consecutive lifetimes are simultaneous lifetimes appearing to be past, present, and future indicating everything is happing in the now!

Chapter 12

Helping Souls Move into the Light

While researching the literature on reincarnation and karma in reference to my four possible cryptomnesia past-life experiences, as well as exploring the concept of simultaneous lifetimes several unexpected doorways opened. In 1989, I began teaching a course on psychic phenomena at the University of Cincinnati's continuing education program. Over the next several years, I became the University's expert on psychic phenomena. I soon began getting referrals from the Psychology Department regarding people who were having haunting experiences. As a result of these referrals, I set up a small research team, which included an Episcopal Priest and psychics to investigate these phenomena.

I soon discovered souls that haunted various locations had not made the transition into the light at death for a variety of reasons. Some souls that died a very violent death were stuck in the locations where they had died. Some souls saw the light but decided not to go into it because they had unfinished business in the earthly realm. For whatever reason, some souls appeared to be lost in the netherworld between the earth plane and the light and did not know they were dead. Many souls were stuck because they were addicted to earthly pleasures such as drugs, alcohol, and sex.

There were also ghostly apparitions that were not souls at all, but astral shells with no soul essence. Astral shells materialized because these souls experienced severe traumas at death and left behind their emotional images imbedded in what Eliphas Levi called astral light (1972, pp. 63, 66-67). According to this view, astral light is the spiritual substance emanating from the upper and lower astral planes, which is an integral part of the imaginal realm that interpenetrates physical reality. Astral planes are areas in spiritual reality manifesting intense feelings and emotions. The upper astral plane manifest positive feeling and emotions, and the lower astral plane manifest negative feeling and emotions. The astral planes exist in the imaginal realm, which encompass the totality of spiritual realities replete with landscapes and animated beings.

Astral light is similar to what quantum mechanics calls quantum foam, which can be molded through thought, measurement or observation. Although, quantum foam is a part of our physical reality, it also interfaces with the spiritual realm. Conversely, astral light is the spiritual equivalent of quantum foam and can be shaped in the spiritual realm through intense emotions both consciously and unconsciously. It appears that astral light and quantum foam can interpenetrate both the spiritual and the physical—everything that exist is part of a grand whole; totally interconnected.

When souls die a violent death, or sudden death, or some other type of tragic death their soul images is fused into the astral light with intense emotions coming from the lower astral plane. These ghostly images are astral shells that have no soul essence or soul identity. These astral shells, as in most ghostly encounters repeatedly reenacts the drama the soul experienced at death, which is always traumatic.

Throughout the period investigating hauntings, our team witnessed many unusual experiences of souls and astral shells that were stuck in the earth plane. These stuck souls and astral shells were creating the haunting manifestations at various locations and needed to be released into the light. In many cases, the Episcopal Priest was able to release these soul identities and move them into the light. However, with astral shells, the priest was able to disintegrate these shadowy soul illusions. As our investigations into hauntings were ending after five years, another unusual case was laid in my lap—twin souls merging.

The twin souls merging case, I spoke about in previous chapters. In this case Jean Cline is the twin soul of the deceased actor George Reeves who played Superman in the 1950s—their souls are attached to each other. Over several years, they began to merge, and she began taking on his physical characteristics. Although they call themselves twin souls, which is how George described their experience, I simply do not believe this phenomenon exists. Most of the people I have worked with that call themselves twin souls, I have diagnosed as psychotic or borderline. However, what I do believe, is Jean and George is a case of dual possession. After extensive psychological assessments, Jean displayed no psychotic characteristics as in other cases I have worked with. Nevertheless, in the Jean and George case, Jean is possessing George's soul and he is possessing her soul, creating the merger. While working with the case for several years, it became evident George was an earth-bound spirit that hadn't gone on into the light, which he admitted later (Cline, Duncan & Coston, 2007).

While working with the Jean and George case, the veil between this world and the spirit world was further lifted. People who I had known personally in life that had passed on began speaking to me. I soon realized working with death, my own death at birth as well as other paranormal phenomena over the years, had opened portals into various landscapes in the afterlife. These doorways allowed me to connect with souls that were either stuck in the netherworld because of unfinished business or wanted to communicate with me for various reasons.

George was stuck in the netherworld because of his ego—wanting to be on stage once again as well as his connection with Jean, all related to unfinished earthly business. The first case I became acquainted with of a soul stuck in the netherworld was when I was a professional member with The Monroe Institute. This organization uses technology called Hemi-Sync, which are binaural sound frequencies to produce altered state of consciousness experiences. Years later, I learned that the Institute had helped a confused and stuck soul move into the light. An Institute facilitator using this technology connected with a man whose ship had sank in the early 1800s. The man was still in the water holding onto a wooden part of the ship and did not know he was dead. The facilitator eventually convinced the man he was dead and was told to look up and he would see a light. He reported he did see the light, and the facilitator finally persuaded him to let go of the wood and go toward the light, which he eventually did.

Working with George around issues of unfinished business, I found myself becoming more open and receptive to souls that had died and were stuck. With George, I could feel his energetic presence at times all around me, he would come into my meditations, and I could see him clearly. These experiences opened the spiritual portals allowing me to feel the soul's energetic presence as well as channels to communicate with the deceased, helping them move on into the light.

The major life-changing experience occurred when an old friend died, the Episcopal Priest, Father Wayland Melton I had known for years, who had been a member of our haunting investigative team. I was distraught for weeks after his death. My melancholy mood suddenly lifted when in the middle of his memorial service, he spoke to me. He said in his voice as if he was speaking to me in life, "This is Wayland, thanks for coming, I'm okay, I'll see you later." I was stunned! This was the first time, anything like that had happened to me. I asked Daryl, my life partner (later my spouse), sitting beside me if he heard Wayland and he said he had not. I was now spiritually open and could not go back to the way things were.

A few years later, my father was diagnosed with lung cancer that metastasized to the brain. I made a conscious decision to set aside specific career goals, and instead listened to his concerns about the dying process and his approaching death. I eventually asked him if any of his loved ones who had died had visited him. He said his mother had visited him several times recently. I knew at that point he would be joining her soon, and he died two weeks later.

However, during one of the last conversations I had with my father he informed me my brother Fred would be arriving in a few days. Fred and I had not seen each other in decades because of my decision not to go into the funeral business and had only spoken briefly in two heated conversations. I knew Fred and Delilah had divorced but did not know he had remarried. In an awkward conversation, my father revealed Fred had remarried and his wife was part African American. I was shocked because when I left my brother decades earlier, he was an ardent racist and bigot. I was pleased Fred had moved away from his deplorable attitudes—people do change. Although he had changed in his bigoted attitudes, the riff between us over the funeral business kept a distance between us that would never heal because of him.

The following Memorial Day, Daryl and I visited my mother, and we all went to the cemetery to decorate my father's grave. I was alone looking at his gravesite, reflecting on the many things we had done in life, then like the experience I had with Wayland, my father spoke to me. In life, when he wanted to get my attention, he would address me by my middle name, "Wayne". In his voice, he said, "Wayne, I'm not there! Wayne, I'm not there!" After that day, I visited his gravesite once, and that was when my mother died. I will never visit his grave again because he told me he was not there.

These afterlife encounters have opened portals between the earth plane and the light, and the landscapes in-between, known as the imaginal realm. These portals have allowed me to connect with the deceased in the afterlife, in ways I never thought possible. Realizing the fullness of the afterlife added richness to my life and has given me a direction to explore my own spirituality further. The experiences with Wayland and my father laid the foundation to work with other departed souls.

After the Memorial Day encounter with my father, my protective armor became diffused, leaving me open to other afterlife experiences. About a year later, Daryl and I were visiting my mother when another life expanding experience flooded into a nightly dream. I had read several biographies of the late actor James Dean and had visited his grave site and hometown in Indiana. While at my mother's, I had a dream of the late actor. Suddenly, the dream narrative shifted, and I found myself in a grayish sepia-tone room. The room looked like a concentration camp barracks with dingy bunk beds, stacked two beds high. On one of the beds was Paul, the childhood and adolescent friend that awakened my sexual orientation when I was seven years old. He had died of a drug overdose a few years earlier. Besides me, he was the only one in the room. He looked gaunt and disheveled lying on a dirty bed. He looked up at me and said, "Gary, where am I?" I told him he was dead, which surprised him.

Thereafter, during meditations, I would work with Paul helping him move out of the place he was in. Together we created a new home for him in the imaginal realm that was bright and sunny, overlooking a beautiful green valley. Paul continued to be with me over the next several years. At times, like with George, I could feel his presence and he would come into my meditations to work on unfinished earthly issues, primarily his drug and alcohol addictions. Then one day, he told me, he was moving on, and thanked me for helping him. I saw Paul in my inner vision walking toward the light and disappeared. I haven't felt his presence, nor has he visited me in my meditations since that day. I feel he is now in a better place in the afterlife.

Shortly after Paul left, another experience came into my meditations; it was my mother. She had died a few years after my father, and I assumed my father was there when she died to welcome her into the light. However, this was not the case. My mother was a deeply religious woman but was convinced she was doomed to hell because of certain thoughts she had. She never revealed what those thoughts were. In the meditation she said, "Gary Wayne, I'm lost." She repeated that over and over. Like my father using my middle name, my mother always referred to me as Gary Wayne. I immediately came out of the meditation. I could not see her but felt her presence and heard her voice.

Knowing she was lost in some darkness, she had created herself because of unfinished business around guilt regarding her thoughts, I began helping her move on. Over the next several weeks during meditations, she would come to me. I told her my father and her mother (my grandmother) were waiting for her in the light. I told her to look for a white door with white light shining all around the edges. It took her a while to find the door and slowly over the next several weeks, I helped her move closer and closer to the door as her fears slowly abated. I continued to reinforce the idea that my father and grandmother were just beyond the door, and all she had to do was open it and go through. I finally convinced her to put her hand on the door handle and that was the last time I heard her and felt her presence.

All the souls who have died that have contacted me I have known in life, and in many cases have had a deep relationship with them. This became evident during the 2009 Christmas holiday season, when another old friend who had died entered my awareness. While sitting watching the fire in the fireplace, a shadowy figure crossed the living room, and then in my inner awareness an image of Greg popped in, with a strong energetic feeling of his presence. Somewhere in the center of my mind, he spoke to me about our last encounter, which wasn't pleasant. I had known Greg for thirteen years. His brother Steph and I had been life-partners for nine years, and finally broke-up. After the breakup, Greg and I remained friends. However, Greg's wife was in constant contact with Steph, which caused insurmountable problems. So, I decided the only way to deal with the issues was to cut off all communication from Greg and his wife.

In spirit, Greg told me he was devastated by my decision to cut off all contact because he felt we were like brothers, and this caused him to go through a severe depression. After he died, he could not move on until we dealt with this unfinished business. Like with Paul and my mother, during meditations Greg would come to me, we worked through our problematic issues and eventually ended with forgiveness. After forgiveness, he told me it was time for him to move on. Like the experience with Paul, I saw Greg walking toward the light and disappeared.

Why did these souls come to me? It was apparent they wanted me to know something specific about their situation. Wayland and my father wanted me to know they were okay. Paul and my mother wanted me to help them out the afterlife situation they had created for themselves. Greg wanted to bring closure to unfinished business between us. My interactions with these souls have confirmed that not all souls go into the light at death. One thing I know without question is there is no death, just a passage from one reality into another. Knowing this, I decided to explore other methods besides meditation that I could use to have a direct connection with the deceased.

In the early 1990s, I had taken several workshops from the Theosophical Society of Ohio. One of the workshops used an imagery method to connect with one's spirit guides. I personally used the method several times with success as well as teaching it to my students at the University of Cincinnati—also with success. However, I had never used it to connect with souls that had crossed over.

I reviewed the method in detail and compared it with the imagery methods I had created earlier to access inner archetypes as well as helping people move into the light. The imagery I finally created to connect with deceased souls was a fusion of the Theosophical imagery method, imagery pathworking methods from Hermetic Order of the Golden Dawn and the Carmelites' imagery technique called Interior Castle. The imagery I finally constructed was long and involved, however, many students did connect with deceased friends and family members. I found those students experiences fascinating because in the imagery they were able to resolve unfinished business between themselves and the deceased.

After many trial-runs with students, I began using the imagery with the bereaved. I would take the bereaved on an imaginary inner journey into the imaginal realm. Deep within the imaginal realm, was a specific thoughtform egregore, which was a large house with a special room used only to communicate with the deceased. The bereaved would decorate the room to their personal taste and specifications. In the room, the deceased and the bereaved would dialogue together resolving unfinished business. I soon discovered the imagery was so successful; I began using it not only in workshops and courses, but in my counseling practice as well. The one major drawback was the imagery was very long and detailed, but the results were always positive in that there was communication between the deceased and the living, and unfinished business was always resolved (see Appendix B, Imagery Long Version).

I had not thought about the length or the intricate details of the imagery until one day visiting an art shop in a nearby town. As I browsed the artwork, a sad shopkeeper asked if I needed help. Within minutes, I discovered her husband had died almost a year earlier and she was still grieving because the death was so sudden, and she was left with many questions unanswered. As a priest, I began consoling her and suddenly, she asked as a priest if I knew of a way, she could contact her husband. The imagery came to mind, but I knew it was too long and involved, but with her deep grief, I had to help. Within minutes, I shortened the imagery to its basic components and a new workable format emerged (see Appendix C, Imagery Short Version).

I told the shopkeeper to find a comfortable place, get very relaxed, and imagine she was standing at the foot of a winding staircase. She would slowly walk up the winding stairs to a second-floor balcony. Facing her was a long hallway with doors on both sides. She would walk down the hallway select one of the doors, open it, walk into an empty room closing the door behind her. She would decorate the room to her choosing; however, the only requirement was to have two comfortable chairs facing each other. She would visualize, focusing on her deceased husband, imagining his features in detail. After visualizing her husband, she would ask him to knock on the door. Hearing the knock, she opens the door, and standing there would be her husband. She invites him in and directs him to one of the two chairs facing each other.

After they sit down, she begins the conversation any way she chooses. The only rule is not to put words into his mouth, allowing him to speak with complete freedom and autonomy. After the visit is completed and questions answered, they get up from the chairs, walk to the door, embrace, and say goodbye. She opens the door for her husband, and he walks away. She then closes the door and stands reflecting on the conversation. She opens the door again, walks out of the room, closing the door behind her, and walks down the hall, down the staircase to the foot of the stairs, and back into her everyday reality. She thanked me and said her prayers had been answered—she now had a way to contact her husband.

Chapter 13

A Soul Returns

Growing up in the racist South, I was influenced by racism all around me. One night in the small two-room house on our property adjacent to the main house, I was playing an old piano. The door unexpectedly opened and there stood a black man whom at first, I didn't recognize. After a few moments, I recognized JC a former high school basketball player that came to our school during integration. At the time, I had no black friends and felt very uncomfortable with him being in my presence.

However, over the next few weeks, James would drop by at night, and we would play the piano together. I was still uncomfortable with him but tolerated the situation. One night, drunk on bourbon and pumped up with racism and hatred from a white neighbor, I was ready for a confrontation. When I came home, I heard the piano playing, opened the door, and there sat JC at the piano with a big smile. A horrible confrontation ensued, and I ran JC off our property with a cacophony of racial slurs. Weeks later, I felt horrendous guilt and shame over the incident, but never saw JC again. Although I never saw him again, the events of that night were instrumental in propelling me to deal with my racism, and the following year, I became part of the civil rights movement.

In November 2011, I was reflecting on various students I had taught over the years. I was thinking about an African American student, I helped work through a bad divorce. Suddenly, another African American replaced his image, a man I had long forgotten, JC. I felt his presence and energy all around me. I simply couldn't shake it. It felt like one of those experiences where you feel a person's presence, or they pop into your mind and shortly thereafter, they call you on the phone.

The feelings were so intense I went to the Internet to try to find him because I wanted to apologize for what I did over fifty years ago. I had no luck, but the feelings persisted. For two days, I felt possessed to find him. Finally, on the third day, I located his sister. She told me he married a woman in Scotland, had two daughters and died there in 1986 of Lou Gehrig's disease. I was stunned! At my request, she sent me a photograph of him.

Since I could not get him out of my mind and felt his intense presence, I decided to take the opportunity to try and heal the spiritual wounds between us. I went through the shortened version of the imagery I had given the shopkeeper in the art store to contact her deceased husband. I used the photograph and my memory to get the physical details of JC's appearance. I decorated the imaginary room to my personal taste and asked him to knock on the door to the room. Suddenly, there was a knock; I opened the door and there stood JC smiling as I last remembered him. I invited him into my special room.

JC and I sat facing each other in front of a fire in the fireplace in deep conversation. Although the conversation began a bit awkward at first because of the guilt and shame I felt, I finally settled into a comfortable repose. Once relaxed, the communication flow took on a life of its own. I soon discovered like Greg, JC had not gone into the light because of unfinished business between us. Over several months, we met in the special room, worked things through and ended with forgiveness. The last time I saw JC, he told me it was time for him to go. We hugged, said goodbye—he walked into the light and disappeared.

The experience with JC motivated me to continue experimenting with the shortened version of the imagery during my morning meditations. Once very relaxed, I would shift my awareness into the special room and attempted to contact other souls as well as spiritual guides. One morning about two years later, I entered the special room and suddenly JC appeared wearing a flowing white hoodless robe—he was back. He said not a word, offered his hand; I put my hand into his and instantly, we were in a different place. He turned to me and said, "Welcome to my inner world."

The structure we were in is hard to describe. It was all white with no doors or windows just large open spaces where a gentle warm breeze continued to circulate through open rooms. The structure looked solid with square support columns; however, the columns were only decorative, they did not support anything; everything appeared to be molded together. The support columns as well as everything in the structure looked like stone. Although looking like hard stone, there was a spongy give to the material when I touched it. Even the tile floor was soft when I walked across it.

JC took me outside and the sky was beautifully white; light was shining everywhere, but there was no sun. There were green rolling hills that went on and on into the distant horizon. When I walked on the grass, it had a soft give to it like everything else—nothing was hard. Behind the structure was a slow-moving river nestled in a valley with a beautiful expanse of green trees, bushes, and grasses.

JC took me back into the structure; we sat down on a white wide and long couch like object with an armrest and a short-curved backrest. There was very little furniture, and it was all white—everything had a glow to it. He told me this is where we can meet between worlds, and then indicated he had come back as my spiritual teacher and protector. Puzzled, I asked, "Protecting me from what?" He explained, because of the work I do helping lost soul's crossover into the light that some of those souls were trying to attach themselves to me, and he is here to shield me and keep me safe. In addition, he said there were still unresolved issues between us to work through, and that surprised me.

Since JC was back in my life, I often entered his thoughtform egregore for brief periods during meditation. In those meditation encounters, I discovered several unique qualities he possesses in the afterlife. He was able to use his conscious intention to create imaginary structures such as the thoughtform egregore as well as the ability to move his soul into many alternative realities—being in many places simultaneously. Within this context, he was able to experience many realities that appeared to exist in the past, present, and future concurrently. This simultaneous connectedness allows his soul to connect not only with me, but with other souls because we are all part of a greater whole, replete with many worlds. The fact that JC's soul is connected with everything and exists everywhere at once as well as existing in many worlds, triggered some insights I had entertained for many years regarding quantum physics and spirituality.

My study of quantum physics began in 1976 when I was in chemical research, and that study has continued to this day. However, in the late 1990s, I began a research project to flesh out how the peculiar properties of quantum mechanics related to spirituality. At the time, I was bewildered by the reality I was living in and began asking two questions I had asked throughout my life, "Why are thing the way they are?" and "Why is there pain and suffering?"

I soon discovered part of the answer was supported by the following quantum properties. Wave/particle duality where two opposites states exist as one state—two sides of the same coin, the foundation for oneness. The observer effect in which the mere fact of observation creates reality by shaping consciousness, creating the reality we live in. Superposition being everywhere at once in which past, present and future exist simultaneously. Entanglement when phenomena are created together or come into existence at the same time, they are forever connected with each other. The many worlds hypothesis in which reality is made up of many worlds or simultaneous realities. All these properties are relevant to spirituality.

Wave/particle duality indicates that all reality exists as a wave and a particle simultaneously. What was most interesting was experiments have shown that waves and particles are not only two manifestations of the same phenomenon, but they are aware of being observed. For example, when a wave is being observed, it collapses into a particle and when the particle is not being observed, it becomes a wave once again. In other words, everything exists as a wave until it is observed or measured at which point, the observation of the wave collapses into particles creating the reality we see around us. In essence, everything that exists on this fundamental level is aware of its reality. Not only is the wave and particle aware of being observed, but they interface with consciousness creating physical reality.

By using his consciousness, JC created the all-white thoughtform egregore we met in. Fundamentally, he used his consciousness by imagining what he desired to manifest and molded astral light or spiritual stuff or quantum stuff into the shape he desired, which was the thoughtform egregore within the imaginal realm. I began questioning, was the thoughtform egregore JC created similar to a computer simulation as in the Matrix movies also known as the simulation hypothesis, although JC did not indicate a computer was involved only his imagination.

All particles, such as electrons, exist as waves in a state of superposition being everywhere at once. When electron waves collapse, they become particles in this case electrons. Superposition is when particles such as electrons exists in all states at once, are everywhere at once and moves on all paths at once—one single electron is all electrons that exist. Although everything exists in superposition being in a state of wave/particle oneness. To change that state into either a wave or a particle depends on how the waves and particles are measured or observed creating the duality we see around us. In other words, we are all part of one grand experience in which everything that exists is entangled with everything else, which means all reality is interconnected; there is no separation between anything. Furthermore, this interconnected wholeness exists in an infinite number of parallel worlds, all waiting to be explored given the right techniques.

As I viewed the quantum implications of JC's experiences, it became evident everything exists both spiritually and physically in quantum reality. In other words, JC's soul exists in many worlds simultaneously both physically and spirituality all within the imaginal realm. He was connected with me from his spiritual reality, which interfaced with me in the physical reality. He created the thoughtform egregore in which we met in from astral light or spiritual stuff or quantum stuff made up of waves and particles. Although JC's thoughtform egregore is not a computer simulation, it is nonetheless some type of thoughtform structure. In the creation of the thoughtform egregore, he used his conscious awareness to manifest the thoughtform egregore by first imagining it in his soul-mind as thought waves and then materializing those thought waves it into particles creating the spiritual thoughtform egregore, we met in.

JC's experiences in the spiritual world fits neatly with quantum reality at the fundamental level. On that fundamental quantum level, I soon learned JC used will power and intention to move the thoughtform egregore from his imagination as waves into the manifestation we experienced. This use of will power is similar to how Sri Aurobindo's used karmic free will to shape his own destiny. In other words, JC used his free will actions to shape quantum/spiritual stuff to build the thoughtform egregore simulation.

In relation to free will and karma, what was surprising was JC indicated will power or karma only affects the actions of our current incarnation and does not follow us from lifetime to lifetime, because our souls are so large, they exist in all realities and lifetimes simultaneously having a variety of experiences. On the topic of karma, JC indicated that what we think of as karmic affects shaping our current lifetimes does not exist, but instead there is information leakage from people we have known that have died that exist in simultaneous lifetimes. We unconsciously allow informational leakage from those deceased people to affect our current lifetime because of unfinished business. He stressed unfinished business from people who have died is the problem—not karma.

As a result of information leakage, lifetimes become conflated, allowing negative information to enter and infect our current life's situations causing mental, emotional, spiritual, and physical pain. Through past-life regressive therapy, an individual moves their awareness into what they perceive as past lives but are only concurrent lifetimes appearing to be past-lives. By re-experiencing aspects of those simultaneous lifetimes with deceased people we have known, our souls fine healing solutions to the unfinished business that is causing us pain.

I discovered concurrent lifetimes could be created with conscious intention because those lifetimes fundamentally are made out of astral light or quantum stuff. Although JC and I had worked through and resolved our past issues, I soon discovered those issues were only partially resolved. To resolve totally the spiritual and emotional pain from that 1960s altercation, a parallel thoughtform egregore had to be constructed out of astral light or quantum stuff alongside the one where the altercation occurred. At first, I was baffled by this idea. However, JC assured me this was the only positive way to completely heal those old wounds, and stop the informational leakage, which was still causing us pain.

With JC in the lead, he took us back to that July night 1967 where the altercation occurred. With his prompting, he changed the scenario. Rather than the racist altercation we had that night, instead, he put into place a new parallel thoughtform egregore in which he began helping me sober up, come to my senses and we ended up as friends. As we continued visiting this new parallel scenario, I became more comfortable with our new friendship, which continued to deepen through joyful conversations and sharing our talents at the piano.

We created a totally differ outcome, essentially a new lifetime, with a separate history. Once the new lifetime was forged, it began to change and evolve. Every time I went to our new thoughtform egregore in my meditations, JC would be waiting, and we began to heal those old wounds by sculpting positive outcomes. I was living in two worlds at once—this world and that world.

In this new lifetime, JC became my constant spiritual companion; we would meet in the new all white thoughtform egregore in the in-between worlds and not in the old 1967 thoughtform egregore. As our conversations evolved, he explained that most of his life while alive was not relevant to our current relationship, and only wanted to focus on our current time together, and not linger on the past. With that revelation, he also added, as our spiritual growth continues to evolve, we needed to create a new lifetime, which I found puzzling.

As before, I allowed him to take the lead and soon the new thoughtform egregore began to materialize out of astral light or quantum stuff. As if watching a movie, our new thoughtform egregore began to emerge all around us as if out of nowhere creating a new lifetime. We were in a contemporary apartment like structure with earthly furnishings very familiar to the physical world I see around me—I felt at home.

The new lifetime was completely separated from all past lifetime experiences with no incarnational baggage leaking in. Moreover, it soon became apparent the new lifetime reflected our current state of spiritual growth. In this new lifetime, we meditated, reflected, and discussed why it's so hard to implement love and compassion in the material world. He indicated the two underlying factors are greed and indifference and once those factors are addressed, we can create a better world molded through positive intentions. We can shape astral light or spiritual stuff or quantum stuff into the world we desired within the limitations of duality, ruled with love, compassion, understanding, forgiveness, and tolerance.

Since the new lifetime had emerged, JC and I met there often to discuss deep spiritual and philosophical questions, mostly revolving around love and compassion. We also discussed how to use will power to mold quantum stuff into our personal physical and spiritual realities. Most of the time, there was no vocal communication between us, only thoughts and emotions being transmitted between us telepathically.

What I was learning from JC was we can change our current lifetime through our imaginative choices. Once we choose a lifetime, we use our imagination to construct it and then use will power and intention to move it from a wave reality into a particle reality, ultimately creating a new life history. He stressed that many lifetimes or parallel realities are created from very low consciousness such as our reality, and information leakage from deceased people we have known seep into our current lifetime, causes major problems. The solution is to create a new lifetime and mold it through imagination, choices, intentions, and actions creating a new personal history.

Consciousness is not only malleable, but is aware, and awareness allows us to choose our destiny and manifest it. Within consciousness, everything is entangled, or interconnected because everything exists in superposition manifesting as a single whole—nothing is separate, everything is interconnected. All realities are entangled and exist within consciousness; some are created consciously and some unconsciously in the imaginal realm accompanied with many thoughtform egregores.

JC's experiences in the afterlife appear to fit with the fundamental properties of quantum mechanics in that he used his imaginative waves to create and materialize new lifetime thoughtforms egregores. According to Sri Aurobindo, karma is a form of free will and if we use this interpretation then JC used free will karma to construct and materialize these thoughtforms egregores.

Also, JC's experiences with free will indicate that the way karma has been taught is inaccurate—there are no karmic debts dooming a person from lifetime to lifetime until those debts are paid. JC's explanation of reincarnation is very different from the traditional view in that there are no consecutive lifetimes. The only lifetimes that exist are simultaneous lifetimes that we can tap into at any time. Because JC's experiences were so different regarding karma and reincarnation, I was glad I had revisited that literature because I now had a better perspective. With a more enlightened view that there is no reincarnation based on karma, only incarnations created by free will.

In addition, I now viewed karma as another name for free will choices, which also have consequences. With this information, I decided to see if JC's communications fit with the body of evidence of near-death-experiences. Because in near-death experiences some souls visit alternative realities appearing free of reincarnation and karma. In addition, are those afterlife realities simply thoughtform egregores created by the experiencer's free will or something else altogether? After intense scrutiny of both thoughtform egregore and simulations, it became apparent they are not simulations, computer or otherwise but thought constructs made from mind constructs both from individuals as well as collective consciousnesses. Bottom line, they are not computer game realities but real spiritual landscapes.

<h1 style="text-align:center">Chapter 14</h1>

NEAR-DEATH EXPERIENCES

JC AND I STAYED IN CONTACT WITH EACH OTHER DURING MY MORNING meditations in the new thoughtform realities he constructed. We continued discussing how our choices creates our personal and collective reality by molding consciousness through intentions into the desired form we choose. Although I had many questions I wanted answered, JC finally indicated our time together was coming to an end. He told me we had worked through all our spiritual issues from that night in 1967. As I watched JC walking toward the light with a big smile, he waved his final goodbye and disappeared; that was several years ago, and he hasn't returned. I often wonder where he is now!

I gained a wealth of information from my connection with JC but the salient feature in his afterlife experience was the creation of thoughtform egregores, which are definitely not computer game simulations. As JC suggested, we construct thoughtform egregores consciously and unconsciously in the imaginal realm, which exists alongside and interpenetrate other realities simultaneously. However, are these thoughtform egregores constructions an integral part of the afterlife experience?

In this context, are the afterlife realities that near-death experiencer's encounter, just thoughtform egregores assembled by advanced spiritual beings similar to JC's constructions? If so, then how does reincarnation and karma fit into these created after death realities. In addition, do people in these near-death thoughtform realities report reincarnation and karmic experiences? Once the soul enters the afterlife do near-death experiencer's have free will like they had in the physical reality or are they affected by karma? Is there evidence in the literature on near-death experience that can answer these questions!

Near-death experiences occur when individuals encounter death, by almost dying, or are pronounced clinically dead and later are brought back to life totally recovered. According to Atwater (2007), near-death experiences are recorded when both the heartbeat and breathing ceases for a period of five to fifteen minutes and in some cases are dead for more than an hour. During these episodes, near-death experiencer's are in a clear vivid state of awareness and understands what is happening to them. Within this cogent state, do these experiencer's perceive their afterlife realities as thoughtform constructions and do they perceive them as real? In addition, within this lucid state can neat-death experiencer's make free will choices to move deeper into their experience or decide to come back to physically reality? Or do karmic debts control these afterlife dramas?

In attempting to understand if free will is involved in the construction of afterlife realities, there does appear to be cases in which the experiencer has free will choices in the afterlife, the in-between life state and in physical reality. In the in-between life experiences (Wambach, 1981), the soul can choose the parents they will be born into, so they can have a particular lifetime experience such as the case reported earlier by Jim Tucker (2005).

It has been reported that Buddhist Lamas called Tulkus choose the time they will die and the parents they will be born into. In Buddhism this is called reincarnation or rebirth. However, the mere fact that there is no karmic debt that keeps the soul tied to the cycle of samsara (pain and suffering) indicates this is not reincarnation in the traditional since, but free will thoughtform constructed incarnations. Remember free will incarnations are situations in which the soul chooses the lifetime experience they desire to have, which is not karmic retribution.

In studying many near-death experience cases, it became clear that some of the world's religious traditions got it wrong—there is simply no reincarnation and karma in the traditional sense and no retribution. In some near-death experience cases a few children do talk about past lives but not like traditional reincarnation with karmic debt. As in the case cited by Tucker (2005, pp.1-3) in a previous chapter in which a man named John chose to incarnate into his grandson William. This transfer of John's soul is like the Buddhist Tulkus in which John chose to come back into this lifetime to help his daughter by incarnating into his grandson William. This is a free will incarnation choice and not karma in which the soul works off some supposed debts from previous lifetimes.

To get a handle on the uniqueness of the near-death phenomena and how it throws retribution into the trash heap of foolish ideas, we need to take a closer look at one of the cases cited in Raymond A. Moody's book Life After Life (p. 74. 1975). This case is similar to other near-death experience (NDE) cases in which there is no foundation for traditional reincarnation, karma, sin or any display of retribution theologies. In this NDE scenario the experiencer relates his experience in detail as it was related to Moody.

> "After a while, he collects himself and becomes more accustomed to his odd condition. He notices that he still has a 'body,' but one of a very different nature and with very different powers from the physical body he has left behind. Soon other things begin to happen. Others come to meet and to help him. He glimpses the spirits of relatives and friends who have already died, and a loving, warm spirit of a kind he has never encountered before—a being of light—appears before him. This being asks him a question, nonverbally, to make him evaluate his life and helps him along by showing him a panoramic, instantaneous playback of the major events of his life. At some point, he finds himself approaching some sort of barrier or border, apparently representing the limit between earthly life and the next life. Yet, he finds that he must go back to the earth, that the time for his death has not yet come. At this point, he resists, for by now he is taken up with his experiences in the afterlife and does not want to return. He is overwhelmed by intense feelings of joy, love, and peace. Despite his attitude, though, he somehow reunites with his physical body and lives. Later he tries to tell others, but he has trouble doing so. In the first place, he can find no human words adequate to describe these unearthly episodes. He also finds that others scoff, so he stops telling other people. Still, the experience affects his life profoundly, especially his views about death and its relationship to life."

As Moody himself points out, it is rare that a person actually goes through every element as he describes it. Rather, his description is a kind of compilation of the most common events. This experience is somewhat different from the forty-nine-day Bardo journey of death and rebirth as experienced in Tibetan Buddhism or the afterlife experience of heaven and hell in Christian theology.

In the above case there is no external judgment of a person's life only the experiencer judges themselves in the life review. In other words, there is no retribution from karmic or sinful deeds and no cyclic reincarnations based on one's earthly actions. These experiences happen to anyone at any age, including newborns and infants. Within this context, near-death experiences can range in content from an out-of-body experience (OBE) to experiencing other worlds and realities, to being in the presence of God or other divine presences and in some cases a void, a darkness or hellish encounter all shaped in some way by the cultures and religions in which one lives.

There are many encounters people have in near-death experiences. To reconfigure Atwater's (2007) description, she explains that some people find themselves in gardens, walking along roads, skipping through lovely pastures, seeing great cities sparkling like jewels, and some experience what it's like to jump on a light beam traveling through the universe as well as plunging into profound darkness.

Moody (1975) identified twenty elements in NDE cases: ineffability that is beyond the limits of any language to describe; hearing yourself pronounced dead; feelings of peace and quiet; hearing unusual noises; seeing a dark tunnel; finding yourself outside your body; meeting spiritual beings; a very bright light experienced as a being of light; a panoramic life review; sensing a border or limit to where you can go; coming back into your body; frustrating attempts to tell others about what happened to you; subtle broadening and deepening of your life afterward; elimination of the fear of death; corroboration of events witnessed while out of your body; a realm where all knowledge exist; cities of light; a realm of bewildered spirits and supernatural rescues.

Although these elements are common, they do not reflect all near-death experiences because no two experiences are identical. However, according to Long and Perry (2010) when many near-death experiences are studied together, a pattern of common elements emerge that occur in consistent order as expressed in the following cases.

Out-of-body experience (OBE), and separation of consciousness from the physical body: "I could feel my spirit actually leaving my body. I saw and heard the conversations between my husband and the doctors taking place outside my room, about forty feet away down a hallway. I was later able to verify this conversation to my shocked husband."

Heightened senses: "It just seemed so much more real than anything I had ever experienced in my entire life." In another case, "More consciousness and alertness than normal." Not only are senses enhanced but intense and generally positive emotions or feelings are experienced, "This is the hardest thing to try and explain…Words will not come close to capturing the feelings, but I'll try: total, unconditional, all-encompassing love, compassion, peace, warmth, safety, belonging, understanding, overwhelming sense of being home, and joy…."

Passing into or through a tunnel: "My next awareness was of being submerged and cradled in a warm, wavy, wafting motion at the opening of a tunnel. The tunnel had billowy soft sides and was well lit, with the tunnel dimensions decreasing and brightness increasing as it got closer to a single bright light."

Encountering a mystical or brilliant light: "At first the light was blue. Then it transitioned to white. It was an opalescent white; it almost glowed but did not shine. It was bright, but not intense bright, like glowing bright-pure bright. Pure but not in the usual sense of the word. Pure as in something you've never seen before or could ever describe or put into words."

Encountering other beings, either mystical beings or deceased relatives or friends: "My dad was right next to me, but I couldn't see him visually. My sister was very close; I felt she was to my left. I felt other family members close by, but I did not see them. My sister and other family members seemed to be more to the left. The only person besides my sister and my dad that I knew was there was my grandmother. There were others there but none I can say for certain besides the ones I mentioned."

A sense of alteration of time or space: "When I first left my body, I had my diving watch on. I took some very unscientific measurements of the distance I traveled by watching for features and measuring them by the second hand on my watch. Totally unscientific. But my conclusion was and has always been I was measuring time in an altered time. The ground never moved in a linear fashion; the distances were erratic at best. The distances were always changing, sometime(s) repeating and then instantly becom(ing) longer or short(er) than the previous distance. Yet my watch was always ticking without change. My intuition and impression were that I was in a different time zone, one where my earth(ly) watch was of no use or inept at making any measurement or reflecting time. Also, without mistake, I would say this whole thing took an hour or more. It seemed to me that I was in the NDE for a very long time. But when I asked my diving partners how long I had been unconscious, they estimated five to ten minutes. Thus, I had another reason to support why my diving watch didn't seem to measure the time in my NDE."

Life review: "Next, he showed me my life review. Every second from birth until death you will see and feel, and [you will] experience your emotions and others that you hurt and feel their pain and emotions. What this is for is so you can see what kind of person you were and how you treated others from another vantage point, and you will be harder on yourself than anyone to judge you."

Encountering unworldly or heavenly realms: "All around me I could see and feel a beautiful peace and tranquility with love and peace .... As far as the eye could see to my left was a beautiful landscape of tulips of every color imaginable. To my right was a wall of a beautiful blue that matched the sky." This description is similar to thoughtform egregores.

Encountering or learning special knowledge: "When I looked into his eyes all the secrets of the universe were revealed to me. I know how everything works because I looked into his eyes for a moment. All the secrets of the universe, all knowledge of all time, everything."

Encountering a boundary or barrier: "I reached the point where I felt I had to make the choice whether to go back to life or onward into death. My best friend was there (who had died of cancer two years before), and she told me that this was as far as I could go, or I would not be able to turn back. 'You have come to the edge. This is as far as you can go,' she said. 'Now go back and live your life fully and fearlessly.'" These boundaries or barriers are similar to thoughtform egregores and computer simulations.

A return to the body, either voluntary or involuntary: "I found out that my purpose now would be to live 'heaven on earth using this new understanding, and also to share this knowledge with other people. However, I had the choice of whether to come back into life or go toward death. I was made to understand that it was not my time, but I always had the choice, and if I chose death, I would not be experiencing a lot of the gifts the rest of my life still held in store. One of the things I wanted to know was that if I chose life, would I have to come back to this sick body, because my body was very, very sick and the organs had stopped functioning. I was then made to understand that if I chose life, my body would heal very quickly. I would see a difference in not months or weeks, but days!'" This account lays out the fact that there is no traditional karma or reincarnation but personal free will choices similar to the John McConnell case and the Buddhist Tulkus.

In general, karma is the belief that an individual's actions determine a person's future situations. This includes the idea that actions in previous lives affect an individual's circumstances in their current life. In view of these NDE accounts, it appears that cyclic reincarnation and karma does not exist as it relates to the work of Ian Stevenson and Jim Tucker. It also appears the soul is told to return to physical reality because it is not time for them to die or the soul choses to return or incarnate back into this physical reality or possibly reborn in some alternate reality. However, what we don't know and cannot know is how many souls choose not to return to physical reality. As some cases indicate, the soul can incarnate into different realities such as parallel worlds or simultaneous lifetimes that could be thoughtforms egregores. Simply put, there is no karma, but free will choices leading to positive or negative consequences in one's life.

Based on this conclusion, it appears that the cases of childhood memories of reincarnation that Stevenson and Tucker documented does not support karma. To reiterate, the traditional understanding of karma is that an individual's circumstances in their current life are thought to be due not just to actions in the last life but also accumulated actions in any of their previous lifetimes. In Tucker's (2005) work this definition was applied to Stevenson's childhood reincarnation cases looking at correlations between present and previous lifetime circumstances.

In Tucker's (2005) evaluation, salient features in the collective database of childhood memories of reincarnation were analyzed to see if there were relationships with any characteristics of the previous personality that would correlate with the characteristics and circumstances in the subject's current lifetime. The questions that were addressed to extract salient features in the previous personality were: Was the previous personality saintly? Was the previous personality a criminal? Did the previous personality commit moral transgressions? Was the previous personality philanthropic or generous? Was the previous personality active in religious observances? These personality features were correlated with the economic and social status as well as the Indian cast status that are present in the person's current lifetime. In this study certain assumptions were made such as a child born to loving supportive parents in poor conditions to be reborn to loving supportive parents in positive conditions. In this context, it can be assumed that positive conditions would be more likely to include higher economic status than lower ones.

When the correlations were analyzed "saintliness" was the only characteristic from the previous personality that correlated with the reincarnated subjects. Saintliness showed a very strong correlation with the economic status of the subjects and a significant correlation with the social status of the subjects. This means the saintlier the previous personality was the higher the economic and social status the reincarnated child was likely to be born into. However, it is interesting that saintliness did not correlate with the caste of the subjects in the Indian cases, and none of the other characteristics of the previous personality correlated with the current circumstances of the subject. Based on these inconclusive results we need to consider that the correlations with saintliness may be a statistical fluke. These correlational results indicate there is little evidence that karma from the previous lifetime affects the current situations in supposed reincarnated subjects.

Another factor in Tucker's (2005) analysis that argues against karmic effects has to do with birthmarks and birth defects. In these cases, current birthmarks and birth defects matches wounds that children remembered suffering in a previous lifetime. If we assume karma, which is action and reaction, was responsible for those birthmarks and birth defects then why would they appear on the subject who suffered from those wounds rather than the person who inflected those wounds? Since this is not the case, we must conclude that these birthmarks and birth defects do not support karma but free will choices on the part of the incarnated subject—they willed them there for whatever reason.

In these cases, through will power, these incarnated subjects like the Buddhist Tukuls chose the parents to incarnate into, and through will power created the birthmarks and birth defects, possibly to prove they lived in a previous lifetime. These are not cases of reincarnation through karma, but simply free will incarnations.

At this point in my exploration and study of the afterlife, which included near-death experiences, reincarnation, and karma, I began to assess how these influences shaped my spiritual life. I no longer believe the traditional view of reincarnation and karma because near-death experiences are more credible than hypnotic past-life regression experiences. In addition, it also appears that will power and free will are the main forces shaping, creating, and manifesting our destiny, through choices and intentions. This is supported by the Copenhagen interpretation of quantum mechanics, in which observation, and measurements create reality.

Throughout my life studying and working with the phenomena of dying, death, the afterlife, and my own death at birth brought me to the realization I am a modern-day spiritual psychopomp. While trying to understand these phenomena and the direction my life was taking, I found myself exploring very esoteric and occult mysteries that lay behind closed doors. These doorways suddenly opened when I found the secret keys to unlock them.

I found myself delving into the mysteries of magick, sexuality, science, religion, and spirituality. Within these mysteries, I discovered portals opening into the vast landscapes of the afterlife and how the soul-spirit (souls that are deceased) transitions from the physical reality crossing the veil into the spiritual reality. Once crossed, the soul-spirits finds themselves in a world of total love and all burdens dissolve, leaving the soul-spirits to experience the oneness with the Ultimate Mind, or the Divine or God, whatever name one chooses to give it. Once the veil was crossed, I was still able to communicate with soul-spirits. Not only were these mysteries shaping my life and my understanding of the afterlife, but my relationship with my spouse Daryl Coston was also having a spiritual impact.

The culmination of all these factors laid a singular pathway to become an Ordained Priest. My journey into priesthood has been affected by the many unusual spiritual experiences and encounters I have had throughout my life. Although becoming a modern-day spiritual psychopomp was the primary unconscious focus at the beginning of my spiritual journey, it wasn't until I became an Ordained Priest that all these streams came together. To understand how all these streams impacted my calling into the priesthood will be chronicled in my next book by revealing how these streams affected my understanding, perceptions, opinions, and conclusions of a larger coherent picture of reality on all levels setting the stage for a very personal encounter with a soul-spirit, my deceased brother-in-law.

It's as if from the very beginning of my spiritual journey, I was destined to become a very different type of priest. However, not an ordinary traditional priest but a calling into the Gnostic Catholic Priesthood. As a Priest, I had the profound realization that religions with all their do's and don'ts and conditions keeps people from connecting and experiencing the Ultimate Mind, or the Divine or God, which is simply unconditional love. In addition, unconditional love is the glue that bonds everything together giving us the sacredness of eternal life. Our souls never die only transformed in the eternal afterlife journey.

Part III

Psychopomp's Tools

Appendix A
Journey into the Light Imagery

Introduction

What follows is the complete script of the Omega Imagery used successfully with terminally ill populations. On occasion, the imagery has also been used with healthy populations. With both populations, the imagery has yielded similar results. Within these populations, the Experiencer is the one guided into the inward journey and the Spiritual Psychopomp is the imagery's guide. The components of the Omega Imagery are music, mindfulness meditation, soul separation from the body, the soul's journey into the Light, soul's brief stay in the Light and the soul's journey back to ordinary reality.

Imagery Setting

The Spiritual Psychopomp creates a relaxing atmosphere by playing the music Inward Harmony by Marcey. In this setting, the Experiencer lies comfortably in a relaxing lounging chair with their arms resting on their thighs or on a bed with their arms by their sides. After the music has been playing for about ten minutes, the Spiritual Psychopomp guides the Experiencer into their imagery journey.

Imagery Script for Individuals

Now close your eyes. Feel your arms relaxed by your side. Feel your body sinking comfortably into the chair (or on the bed). Just relax and let go of all thought and let all tensions fade away...Pause...Now focus your attention on your breath...Pause...Observe your breath going into your lungs and your breath going out of your lungs. As you breathe, become aware of your abdomen rising and falling with each in-breath and with each out-breath...Pause...Just continue for a few minutes watching your breaths going in...and watching your breaths going out and watching your abdomen rising and falling.

Allow the Experiencer to be in this state of mindfulness meditation for about five minutes.

Now relax... and as you relax... watching your breaths going into your lungs... and your breaths going out of your lungs... and the rising and falling of your abdomen. Now focus your attention on what I'm saying and only on what I'm saying. You have a soul-body that is attached to your physical body. Your soul-body and physical body are energized and animated by the life force of the Spirit. Now become aware of your physical body... Notice if there are any stresses and tensions in your physical body... If there are...just relax more and more and breathe slowly allowing the stresses and all tensions just to fade away with each in-breath and with each out-breath. Take a minute and feel the sensations of your physical body... Become aware of the sounds of your physical body. How does your physical body sound? Now become aware of how your physical body is sitting in the chair (or lying on the bed). Are there any discomforts in the way you are sitting (or laying) ...? If so... reposition your physical body to become more comfortable.

Now become aware you have a second body that energetically interpenetrates and surrounds your physical body. Your physical body is comfortably secure... embedded and engulfed within this second body. Now notice how this second body fits tightly within your physical body... as well as outside of your physical body... This second body is your soul-body. You can feel the life energy from the Spirit subtlety pulsating, surging, and interpenetrating throughout your physical body and throughout your soul-body. This pulsating, surging and interpenetrating life energy keeps your physical body and your soul-body attached... Your physical body feels alive, strong, and solid... and your soul-body feels alive, energetic, and light.

Now you are your soul-body… and your soul-body is beginning to detach both from the inside and from the outside of your physical body. You are now inwardly aware and observing your soul-body disconnecting from your physical body… Now your soul-body has disconnected from your physical body. Although your soul-body is disconnected from your physical body… the Spirit's life energy still surrounds and continues to flow into your physical body and into your soul-body. Your soul-body is now moving from the inside of your physical body and from the outside of your physical body. Your soul-body is now moving toward and accumulating at the top of your head… Now your soul-body is moving out and away from your physical body… it is moving through the top of your head… Your soul-body is now out of your physical body. Your awareness is now in your soul-body… You can now observe your physical body lying comfortably in the chair (or on the bed).

Your awareness is now totally in your soul-body… You are now aware of the room you are in… from the viewpoint of your soul-body floating above your physical body. Your soul-body is now moving up, up toward the ceiling and you can see the room in all directions at once. Your soul-body is now moving through the ceiling… You can see layers of paint… layers of plasterboard and the spaces created by the wooden joists between the ceiling and the floor above… You can see the subfloor, the grains in the wood of the subfloor… You can now see the wood attached on top of the subfloor… You can now see the carpet lying on the wood floor.

Depending on the building, reframe the imagery to accommodate the type of building structure the imagery is performed in. If there are several floors account for the number of floors. Account for the type of floor, such as if the floor is hardwood or carpeted or if the floor is concrete. If the structure is concrete account for the concrete layout, if wood, account for the wood layout. If the roof is flat, arched, or angled account for the design.

Now you are moving upward through the second-floor room (if there is a second-floor)… You can see the entire room from all directions at once… You can see the room's furnishings as you move upward toward the ceiling. Your soul-body is moving up, up through the room and you are now at the ceiling… Your soul-body is now moving through the ceiling… You can see layers of paint and layers of plasterboard as you move into the loft… You see the wooden joists the ceiling is attached to. You see the insulation lying between the joists. You see the angled slant of the interior roof of the loft… You see the wooden studs supporting the roof of the house (or building) … Your soul-body is now passing through the roof. You can see the wood grain. You can see the layered shingles (or roofing such a tarpaper) as you pass through. Your soul-body is now outside the house (or building) … You are seeing the outside world. You are now standing outside on the roof.

There are two beings of light standing on the roof waiting for you… One being of light is standing on your right side and takes your right hand into theirs. The second being of light is standing on your left side and takes your left hand into theirs… The two beings of light are now escorting you toward a small dot of bright light… You are now moving toward the small dot of bright light… You notice the only thing you can see… is the small dot of bright light ahead of you. As you move toward the small dot of bright light… you can now see more details of the dot of light as you move toward it. Your soul is now moving closer and closer to the dot of bright light… The dot of light is now getting larger and larger and brighter and brighter… The brightness of the light does not affect you in any way… as you look directly into it. You notice the light is intensely bright… but very soft, warm, secure, comfortable, and filled with love.

You are now in the light… bathed in feelings of immense unconditional love. Love beyond any love you have ever experienced in your lifetime. The two beings of light let go of your hands and moves aside. You now stand immersed in a sea of love… Your loved ones who have passed on are now all around you… You will be in the light with your loved ones for about thirty minutes. After you have communicated with your loved ones for thirty minutes, the beings of light will guide you back to your physical body.

After the Experiencer has been in the light for about thirty minutes, the Spiritual Psychopomp guides them back to their physical body in ordinary reality.

It is now time for you to say goodbye to your loved ones… Now turn away from your loved ones and there standing by your side are the two beings of light… One being of light takes your right hand into theirs and the second being of light takes your left into theirs… You are now moving away from the bright light… back toward your physical body… You now see a subtle light ahead of you… You are moving toward the subtle light. The light you are moving toward is very different from the light you are moving away from… The light you are moving toward is not as bright and is less intense… It is the light of the material world… where your physical body is lying comfortably waiting for your return.

You are now being escorted by the two beings of light toward your physical body… You are now seeing the roof of the house where you first met the beings of light. Now the beings of light gently bring you back to the roof of the house (or building). You are now standing on the roof… The two beings of light let go of your hands. You now watch the two beings of light ascend back toward the bright dot of light and vanish.

You are now descending back down through the roof. You see the angled rafters of the interior of the roof… You are descending through the loft and through the insulation between the joists… You now see the plasterboard and the layers of paint on the ceiling as you descend into the upstairs room… You see the room from all directions. You see the furnishings in the room as you move down toward the floor… You are now moving through the floor. You see the carpet… You see the wood grain of floor the carpet is laying on… You see the grain in the wood (or concrete) of the subfloor as you pass through the floor descending down and down… You now see the space created by the floor joist. As you move downward… you see the layered plasterboard. You see the layered paint. You are now through the ceiling into the next room. You see all the furnishing in the room… You see the room in all direction… You look down and see your physical body lying comfortably in the chair (or bed).

You move down… down toward your physical body…you as a soul-body now touches the top of your head. Your soul-body now enters your physical body… You feel your soul-body now reconnecting with your physical body. You now become one with your physical body…both on the inside and the outside. Your physical body is now comfortably embedded and secure within your soul-body… Your soul-body and your physical body are now totally re-connected. Life energy is continuing to flow from the Spirit…Life energy from the Spirit is flowing throughout your soul-body and your physical body.

On the count from ten to one, you will come back to this room. You are feeling very relaxed, centered, in a state of harmony and feeing totally loved. Ten, nine, eight…you are slowly coming back to ordinary reality…seven, six, five…you are almost back to ordinary reality…four, three, two, one…you are back. Open your eyes and come back to this room.

Allow the Experiencer time to readjust to ordinary reality. Once back to ordinary reality, the experience is processed. The Spiritual Psychopomp asked the Experiencer what they experienced while they were in the light. The Spiritual Psychopomp does not make any judgments on either the experience, interpretation or the meaning the Experiencer attaches to the experience.

Appendix B
IMAGERY TO CONNECT WITH THE DECEASED IN THE IMAGINAL REALM

Long Version

Relax and move into a mindfulness meditation.... Close your eyes.... Focus on your breath coming into your lungs...and your breath going out of your lungs.... As you focus on your breath...you will notice you are becoming more and more relaxed...both in your mind and in your body.... As your body relaxes...you will notice your mind becoming very still and clear.... Once your body is relaxed...and your mind is clear...and active thoughts have slowed to a calm pace...move into an active state of imagination.

Imagine it's a bright sunny day...and you are leisurely walking down a pathway that's aligned with green grass and wildflowers... As you walk...you become aware of a few trees draping over the pathway.... As the sun makes its way through the tree limbs...it warms your face and body.... You notice one of the trees is loaded with beautiful shiny deep red apples.... You stop...and pluck an apple from the tree...you smell it...it has a deep rich aroma... You feel the apple's smooth textured surface...and you bring it up to your mouth... You bite into the apple...and the juice splatters on your face... Your palate detects the apple's sweet/tart taste...it's delicious.

After taking a few bites of the apple...you continue on your journey.... The sky is blue with a few low hanging fluffy white clouds...floating effortlessly across the bright shinny powder-blue background.... The pathway gingerly moves down a small hill…into a clover laden meadow… You take a slow deep relaxing breath…inhaling the aroma of the clover fragrant setting…. With each step you take…you become more and more relaxed…you hear the soft sweet songs of birds…as they fly from tree to tree.

You continue walking along the pathway…it suddenly moves to the left… and straight ahead is an old stone bridge that arches in the middle…. Walking on old stone bridge…you notice the sides of the bridge are waist-high…with small decorative rounded stones on top…creating a handrail…. As you walk on the bridge…you stop at the apex of the arch…and turn to the right facing the water below…. Putting your hands on the rough round stone top of the bridge's handrail…you stand staring into the pristine crystal-clear water below.

Staring into the water…you notice green grass carpeting the riverbank below…growing down to the water's edge…. You notice the water meandering on and on into the distant horizon…. A few tree limbs bow over the slow-moving water…casting shimmering shadows…reflecting the water's depth…. A few fish jump out of the water…and splash back in again…. You notice the water rippling in concentric circles…created by the fish…as your thoughts focuses on questions about your life…past…present and future…. Questions you have had for many years…about who you are…and where you're going with your life.

You take your hands off the bridge's round stone handrail…turn left…and continue on your journey…. As you cross the bridge…you see two pillars at the end of the bridge…on each side of the pathway…. The pillar on the right is white…and the pillar on the left is black…balancing the opposites in the physical world…. You relaxingly approach the two pillars…and suddenly feel a burst of energy that surges throughout your body…. Not only do you feel energized…but you feel connected with all of creation…. The energy…propels you through the two pillars…leaving physical reality behind.

As soon as you are through the two pillars…you are now deep in the imaginal realm…. Up ahead…you see a large white pillared two-storied house…. You continue walking up the pathway…to the three steps…leading up to porch…. You walk up the three steps…crossing the porch to the large ornate front door…. The door is made of light oak…and blemished with age…. You put your hand on the brass decorative levered door handle…pushing it down… and open the door.

In front of you…is a large entrance hall…leading to a winding staircase… You walk over to the staircase…and slowly walk up the winding stairs…noticing the decorative paisley rose color wallpaper to your left…and a chandelier suspended from the ceiling to your right…. You continue walking up the steps…to the second-floor balcony…. You turn left…and facing you…is a long hallway with doors on both sides…. You slowly walk down the hallway…and select one of the doors.

You stand facing the door…noticing it too…is made of oak…and also has a brass levered door handle…. You put your hand on the door handle…and push down…and open the door…. Facing you is an empty room…. You walk in the room…and close the door behind you.

This room will be your inner sanctuary…. In the next several minutes… decorate the room creating your inner sanctuary…. Decorate your inner sanctuary any way you choose…adding sacred objects…such as an altar… sacred images…such as holy figures…. Put windows anywhere you choose… overlooking a sacred garden… Add any type of furnishings…. Decorate the walls…in any style you like…. The only requirement is there needs to be two comfortable chairs…facing each other.

Your inner sanctuary is now decorated…. Visualize and focus…on the deceased loved one you wish to communicate with…. In the next couple of minutes…bring their image…with all their physical details…you remember into view….in your inner awareness…. Their image is now firmly in your mind… asked them to knock on the door to your inner shrine…. Hearing the knock on the door…. You open the door…and there standing is the loved one…you visualized and focused on… You invite them into your inner sanctuary…and direct them to one of the two chairs facing each other.

After your loved one sits down…you sit in the opposite chair…. Once comfortable…you begin the conversation…any way you wish…. The only rule…is do not put words into their mouth…allow them to speak with complete free-will and autonomy… You may hear things…you like…and you may hear things…you do not like…. You have fifteen minutes to converse with your loved one…and after that period of time…I will lead you on your journey… back to physical reality.

It is now time…to say goodbye….to you loved one…. You get up from your chairs…and walk your loved one over to the door…. You open the door and turn…face to face…with your loved one…. You embrace them and tell them goodbye…until you meet them again…in your inner sanctuary…. They turn and walk away…. You close the door…and stand reflecting on the conversation…you have just had…. You take a slow deep breath…and open the door…. You walk out of your inner sanctuary…closing the door behind you.

You walk down the hallway to the balcony…. You turn right and walk down the winding staircase…to the entrance hall…. You cross the entrance hall…to the large oak front door…. You open it…and cross the threshold to the porch…and close the door behind you…. You walk across the porch to the three steps…. You walk down the steps…to the pathway.

You turn toward the house…taking a last long reflective look…. You turn…and walk toward the two pillars…standing on each side of the pathway…to the entrance to the stone bridge…. The pillars are now reversed…the one on the right is now black…and the pillar on the left is now white…. You walk up to the two pillars…that lead you back into physical reality…. You walk through the pillars…and again feel a burst of energy…that surges throughout your body…connecting you to the whole of creation…. The energy propels you through the two pillars…leaving the imaginal realm behind… . You are suddenly back…in physical reality…standing on the bridge.

You walk to the middle of the bridge…and again…stand at the apex…. You turn left…put your hands on the bridge's round stone handrail…and stair into the water below….as it meanders on and on…into the distant horizon… . You reflect on the experience…you have just had with your love one.

You take your hands off the stone bridge handrail…and continue walking along the pathway…. The pathway turns right…and you find yourself in the clover-laden meadow…smelling the subtle sweetness of the relaxing fragrances…. You continue walking on the pathway…and up the small hill…. Walking up the small hill…you again notice the beautiful sunny powder-blue sky…you walk past the apple tree…hearing the birds chirping their daily songs…. You notice the beautiful green grass…and the fragrant flowers… aligning the pathway…where you began your journey.

On the count from ten to one…you will come back to this room…. You are feeling very relaxed…centered…in a state of harmony…and feeling totally loved…. Ten…nine…eight…you are slowly becoming aware of the presence of this room…you are slowly coming back to ordinary reality…. Seven…six…

five…. Get in touch with the smells…. Get in touch with the sounds…. You are almost back to ordinary reality…. Four…three… two…. Get in touch with the pressure…sitting on the chair… Get in touch with your feet on the floor… . Get in touch with the taste in your mouth…. Get in touch with the light coming through your eyelids…. One…you are back…to ordinary reality…. Now slowly open your eyes…and slowly come back to this room…. Stand up…and shake your arms…and hands…and stamp your feet on the floor…to reground yourself…back in the physical reality.

Appendix C
Imagery to Connect with the Deceased in the Imaginal Realm

Short Version

You are looking at a large white pillared two-storied house…. You walk up to three steps…leading to the porch…. You walk up the three steps…crossing the porch to the large ornate front door…. The door is made of light oak… and blemished with age…. You put your hand on the brass decorative levered door handle…pushing it down…and open the door.

In front of you…is a large entrance hall…leading to a winding staircase… You walk over to the staircase…and slowly walk up the winding stairs…noticing the decorative paisley rose color wallpaper to your left…and a chandelier suspended from the ceiling to your right…. You continue walking up the steps…to the second-floor balcony…. You turn left…and facing you…is a long hallway with doors on both sides…. You slowly walk down the hallway…and select one of the doors.

You stand facing the door…noticing it too…is made of oak…and also has a brass levered door handle…. You put your hand on the door handle…and push down…and open the door…. Facing you is an empty room…. You walk in the room…and close the door behind you.

This room will be your inner sanctuary…. In the next several minutes… decorate your inner sanctuary any way you choose… Add any type of furnishings…. Decorate the walls…in any style you like…. The only requirement is there needs to be two comfortable chairs…facing each other.

Your inner sanctuary is now decorated…. Visualize and focus…on the deceased loved one you wish to communicate with…. In the next couple of minutes…bring their image…with all their physical details…you remember into view….in your inner awareness…. Their image is now firmly in your mind…asked them to knock on the door to your inner sanctuary…. Hearing the knock on the door…. You open the door…and there standing is the loved one…you visualized and focused on… You invite them into your inner sanctuary…and direct them to one of the two chairs facing each other.

After your loved one sits down…you sit in the opposite chair…. Once comfortable…you begin the conversation…any way you wish…. The only rule…is do not put words into their mouth…allow them to speak with complete free-will and autonomy… You may hear things…you like…and you may hear things…you do not like…. Converse with your loved one as long as you like.

After your questions have been answered…. It is now time…to say goodbye….to you loved one…. You get up from your chairs…and walk your loved one over to the door…. You open the door and turn…face to face…with your loved one…. You embrace them and tell them you love them…then say goodbye…until you meet them again…in your inner sanctuary…. They turn and walk away…. You close the door…and stand reflecting on the conversation…you have just had…. You take a slow deep breath…and open the door…. You walk out of your inner sanctuary…closing the door behind you.

You walk down the hallway to the balcony…. You turn right and walk down the winding staircase…to the entrance hall…. You cross the entrance hall…to the large oak front door…. You open it…and cross the threshold to the porch…and close the door behind you…. You walk across the porch to the three steps…. You walk down the steps…that lead you back into physical reality

On the count from ten to one…you will come back to this room…. You are feeling very relaxed…centered…in a state of harmony…and feeling totally loved…. Ten…nine…eight…you are slowly becoming aware of the presence of this room…you are slowly coming back to ordinary reality…. Seven…six… five…. Get in touch with the smells…. Get in touch with the sounds…. You are almost back to ordinary reality…. Four…three… two…. Get in touch with the pressure…sitting on the chair… Get in touch with your feet on the floor…

. Get in touch with the taste in your mouth…. Get in touch with the light coming through your eyelids…. One…you are back…to ordinary reality…. Now slowly open your eyes…and slowly come back to this room…. Stand up…and shake your arms…and hands…and stamp your feet on the floor…to reground yourself…back in the physical reality.

REFERENCES

Ashcroft-Nowicki, D. (1992). The New Book of the Dead. Northampton: Great Britain. Aquarian.

Atwater, P. M. H. (2007). The Big Book of Near-Death Experiences. Charlottesville: VA. Hampton Roads.

Aurobindo, S. (2007). The Integral Yoga. Twin Lakes: WI. Lotus. — (1952 / 1991). Rebirth and Karma. Lotus.

Becker, Ernest (1973). Denial of Death New. New York: NY. Simon & Schuster.

Bernstein, Morey. (1965). The Search for Bridey Murphy. New York: NY. Doubleday.

Blackman, S. (2005). Graceful Exits. Boston: MA. Shambhala.

Bletzer, J. G. (1987). The Donning International Encyclopedic Psychic Dictionary. Norfolk: VA. Donning.

Blavatsky, H. P. (1972). Isis Unveiled. Wheaton: IL. Theosophical. — (1972/1997, p. 87). Isis Unveiled: Secrets of the Ancient Wisdom Traditions, Madame

Blavatsky's First Work. In Michael Gomes' A New   Abridgment for Today. Wheaton: IL. Quest.

Budge, W. (1960). The Book of the Dead. New York: NY. Bell.

Chadwick, G. (1988). Discovering Your Past Lives. Chicago: IL. Contemporary.

Cherry, Kittredge. (Aug 28, 2021). Augustine of Hippo: Saint who rejected his bisexual past, defended intersex people. In St. Augustine Confessions, Book 4. 4-6). https://qspirit.net/Augustine-hippo-queer-saint/

Corbin, Henry. (1972, Spring). Mundus Imaginalis or the Imaginary and the Imaginal. An Annuel of Archetypal Psychology and Jungian Thought. New York: NY. Spring.

Cline, Jean A., Duncan, Gary W. and Coston, Daryl I. (2007). Twin Souls Merging. South Berwick: ME. Jillett.

Delaforge, Gaetan. (1988, No. 6, Winter, pp. 8-13). The Templar Tradition Yesterday and Today. Gnosis Magazine.

De Laurence, L. W. (1914). The Greater Key of Solomon. Chicago: IL. De Laurence. — (1916). The Lesser Key of Solomon Goetia: The Book of Evil Spirits. Chicago: IL. De Laurence.

Duncan, Gary W. (Jan.-Feb. 2014). Twin Souls Merging, Another Look. New Dawn Magazine.

— (2014, No. 143, March-April pp. 65-70). Helping Stuck Souls Crossover. New Dawn.

— (Special Issue, Vol. 9, No. 6, Special Issue, pp. 35). Making Contact in the Imaginal Realm. New Dawn.

— (Special Issue, Vol. 10, No. 3, pp. 19). Inhabitants of the Imaginal Realm. New Dawn.

Hamm, Marcey. (1986). Inward Harmony (Musical composition). Richardson: TX. Music by Marcey.

Head, Joseph and Cranston, Sylvia. (1977). Reincarnation: The Phoenix Fire Mystery. San Diego, CA. Point Loma.

David-Neel, A. (1932). Magic and Mystery in Tibet. New York: NY. Dover.

— (1997), Immortality & Reincarnation. Rochester: VT. Inner Traditions.

Dale. C. (2008). Illuminating the Afterlife. Boulder: CO. Sounds True. Epic of Gilgamesh. (2100 BCE, Tablet VII and VIII). https://www.sparknotes.com/lit/gilgamesh/mini-essays

Evans-Wentz, W. Y. (1975). Tibetan Book of the Dead (Third Edition). New York: NY. Oxford University.

Feuerstein, G. (1990). Encyclopedic Dictionary of Yoga. New York: NY. Paragon.

Feinstein, D. and Mayo, P. E. (1990). Rituals for Living and Dying. New York: NY. Harper Collins.

Foos-Graber, A. (2007). Deathing. York Beach: ME. Nicolas-Hays.

Goodrich-Clarke, N. (2004, p. 16). Western Esoteric Masters Series: Helena Blavatsky. Berkley: CA. North Atlantic.

Hamilton- Parker, C. (2001). What to Do When You Are Dead. New York: NY. Sterling.

Harding, D. E. (1988). The Little Book of Life and Death. New York: NY. Arkana.

Head, J. & Cranston, S. (1961/1985). Reincarnation: An East-West Anthology. Wheaton: IL. Quest.
— (1977, reprint 1991). Reincarnation: The Phoenix Fire Mystery. San Diageo: CA. Point Loma.

Hudson, T. J. (1893), The Law of Psychic Phenomena. Chicago: IL. A. C. McClurg. CA. Point Loma.

Johnsen, Linda. (2012), Reshaping the Future: Yogic Tools to Alter Your Destiny. Light of Consciousness. Vol. 23, Number 2, p. 10.

Jones, J. P. (2007). Light on Death. New York: NY. Mandala.

Klimczak, Natalia. (July 2016). https://www.ancient-origins.net/history-ancient-traditions/what-was-real-relationship-between-alexander-great-and-hephaestion-006263

Kramer, K. (1988). The Sacred Art of Dying. Mahwah: NJ. Paulist.

Levi, Eliphas. (1972). Transcendental Magic. New York: NY. Samuel Weiser.

Lommel, P. V. (2010, p. 324). Consciousness Beyond Life: The Science of Near-Death-Experience. New York: NY. Harper.

Long, Jeffrey and Perry, Paul. (2011). Evidence of the Afterlife: The Science of Near Death Experience. San Francisco: CA. Harper One.

Monroe, Robert A. (1971). Journeys Out of The Body. New York: NY. Doubleday.

Moody, R. A. (1975). Life After Life. St. Simons: GA. Mockingbird. New York: NY. Free Press.

Moody, R. A. and Perry, P. (1993). Reunions. New York: NY. Villard.

Mumford, J. (1999). Death Beginning or End? St. Paul: MN. Llewellyn.

Matthews, Bruce. (1986, pp.123-144). Post-Classical Developments in the

Concepts of Karma and Rebirth in Theravada Buddhism. In Ronald W. Neufeldt Editor) Karma and Rebirth: Post Classical Developments. Albany: NY. State University of New York Press.

Neiman, C. and Goldman, E. (1994). Afterlife. New York: NY. Viking.

Newton, M. (1996). Journey of Souls. St. Paul: MN. Llewellyn.

Osis, Karlis. (1979). At the Hour of Death. New York: NY. Avon.

Padmasambhava. (2006). The Tibetan Book of the Dead. New York: NY. Viking. Personal relationships of Alexander the Great. https://en.wikipedia.org/wiki/Personal_relationships_of_Alexander_the_Great

Ponlop. D. (2008). Mind Beyond Death. Ithaca: NY. Snow Lion.

Reese, W. L. (1996) Dictionary of Philosophy and Religion: Eastern and Western Traditions. Amherst: NY. Humanity

Richelieu, Peter. (1952/1989). A Soul's Journey. Great Britain. Aquarian.

Rinar, T. (2005). Journey Home. New York: NY. O Books

Rinpoche, S. (1994). The Tibetan Book of Living and Dying. San Francisco: CA. Harper.

Tart. C. T. (2009). The End of Materialism: How Evidence of the Paranormal is Bringing Science and Spirit Together. Oakland: CA. New Harbinger. The Dalai Lama. (2005). The Tibetan Book of the Dead. New York: NY. Viking. The Death of Enkidu. (2100 BCE, Tablet VII and VIII). https://arthistoryproject.com/timeline/the-ancient-world/mesopotamia/the-epic-of-gilgamesh/gilgamesh-3-the-death-of-enkidu/

Thich, N. H. (2002). No Death No Fear. New York: NY. Riverhead.

Thondup, T. (2006). Peaceful Death Joyful Rebirth. Boston: MA. Shambhala.

Starhawk. (1997). The Pagan Book of Living and Dying. New York: NY. Harper Collins.

Storm, Howard. (2000/2005). My Decent into Death: A Second Chance at Life. New York: NY.

Sudduth, M. (2009). Super-Psi and the Survivalist Interpretation of Mediumship. Journal of Scientific Exploration. Vol. 23, No 2, pp. 167-193.

Tucker, Jim B., M.D. (2008). Life Before Life: Children's Memories of Previous Lives. New York: NY. St. Martin's Griffin.

Wambach, H. (1981). Life Before Life. New York: NY. Bantam.

Wikipedia. Cryptomnesia. https://en.wikipedia.org/wiki/Cryptomnesia

Williams, Yona. (August 7, 2008). The Loves of Alexander the Great, Hephaestion & Campaspe. American Civilizations. https://www.unexplainable.net/ancients/the-loves-of-alexander-the-great-hephaestion-campaspe.php

Willis, Janice Dean (1972). The Dimond Light: An Introduction to Tibetan Buddhist Meditations. New York: NY. Touchstone.

Yogananda, P. (1946/2001). Autobiography of a Yogi. Los Angeles: CA. Self-Realization Fellowship.

— (1982/2008, p. 434). Man's Eternal Quest: Collected Talks & Essays on Realizing God in Daily Life, Vol. 1. Los Angeles: CA. Self-Realization Fellowship.

Zaleski, C. (1987). Otherworld Journeys. New York: NY. Oxford.

Zeland, Vadim. (2012). Reality Transurfing, Steps I-V. OJSC Ves Publishing Group.